£1·45

The Topical Times

CONTENTS

All first-person articles as told to " Topical Times Football Book " writers

D. C. Thomson & Co., Ltd.   London : Manchester : Glasgow : Dundee

FOOTBALL BOOK

RAY CLEMENCE
Liverpool

TREVOR BROOKING
West Ham and England

ARSI

The team that missed out...and Pat Rice

IN just nine days the Arsenal season fell apart. On May 10 they went to Wembley for a record breaking 'hat-trick' of F.A. Cup final appearances—and lost 1-0 to West Ham United.

Five days later they went to Brussels to meet Valencia, of Spain, in the final of the European Cup Winners' Cup. It was 0-0 after 90 minutes and still 0-0 after extra time. So it was on to penalties. Five penalty shots to each side.

Mario Kempes, the Argentine World Cup star, stepped forward to take the first—and missed.

Then Liam Brady, with a chance to put all the tension on the Spanish side, missed with his shot.

Solsona, Pablo, Castellanos and Bonhof scored for Valencia. Matched by Stapleton, Sunderland, Talbot and Hollins for Arsenal. All square at 4-4.

Arias stepped forward for the Spanish side and scored. Graham Rix went next for Arsenal—and saw his shot saved.

The Gunners had lost the trophy by 5-4 on spot-kicks. It left Rix in tears with skipper Pat Rice leading the charge of Arsenal players to console their team mate.

It left Arsenal needing to beat Wolverhampton and Middlesbrough to qualify for the current season in Europe.

Two days after their dramatic game in Brussels they beat Wolves. Three days later they lost 5-0 to Middlesbrough! The Gunners started the current season with nothing on the Highbury trophy table, and not even a place in Europe. And that after a season when they could have finished as double cup winners, a term to match the League and F.A. Cup season of 1970-71.

You had to be around in Brussels, Wolverhampton and Middlesbrough to appreciate the spirit of this Arsenal side.

Putting a brave face on Arsenal's failure in Brussels was skipper Pat Rice, the lone survivor of the Arsenal side that won the League and F.A. Cup.

A player who had set up a new record by appearing in five Wembley F.A. Cup finals with the same club and who is the perfect example to any schoolboy who wants to become a professional footballer by hard work and application.

Born in Belfast, Pat moved with his family to Islington as a ten-year-old. Lived within strolling distance of the Highbury ground and won a place in the Arsenal side because he would never give up.

He was turned down by Islington schoolboys, but was invited to train twice a week at Highbury. In his early days he was kept on for his enthusiasm alone.

Living just around the corner from Highbury, he would go back in the afternoons and work on any weaknesses in his game. Trying to get a left foot to match his natural right 'peg'. Improving his heading ability.

Early on there were question marks about his ability to reach the top Arsenal standards. But always he was willing to learn, and now he ranks with any of the very big names that have come out of Highbury.

Over the years there have been so many players with natural ability who have failed because of lack of effort.

Joy for Arsenal. Brian Talbot celebrates after scoring the goal that beat Liverpool in the semi-final of the Cup.

Pat Rice bridged the gap because he was always willing to train and work hard.

Probably the best example to any youngster who is determined to make progress and become a professional footballer.

"I never stop working at my game," he says.

It's an attitude that Pat Rice took with him to Highbury as a schoolboy and one of the reasons why Arsenal have got over the disappointments of last season.

"We'll just have to do it all over again in the current season," says Pat Rice. "And make sure that we win this time."

ENAL
—the skipper who's leading the fight-back

The ups and downs of a long, hard season mirrored in the face of Pat Rice

GERRY FRANCIS (No. 8) hits the deck in a clash with Ipswich 'keeper PAUL COOPER. RUSSELL OSMAN, Ipswich, stands by.

Close Encounters!

All in a tangle are ALAN GOWLING, Bolton (left) and MARTIN PETERS, Norwich.

DAVID O'LEARY, Arsenal, tackled by TONY GALVIN, Spurs.

KEN McNAUGHT, Villa, outjumps JUSTIN FASHANU, Norwich.

Coming to grips are (left) PHIL NEAL, Liverpool and Birmingham's ALAN AINSCOW.

The ball must be won—that's the message from these pictures of tussles for possession

GRAEME SOUNESS, Liverpool, takes it lying down as he tackles Arsenal's JOHN HOLLINS.

11

CLOSE-UP ON CLOUGH

HOW THE CLOUGH-TAYLOR TEAM TACKLE THE TRANSFER MARKET

NOTTINGHAM FOREST manager Brian Clough was the first English boss to spend a million pounds on one player, when he bought Trevor Francis from Birmingham City.

Francis repaid some of the money by scoring Forest's winning goal in the 1979 European Cup final. But a year later Forest were busy negotiating his transfer to the Spanish club Barcelona for a fee of £1½ million.

The figures dazzle the eye but Brian Clough and his partner Peter Taylor view spectacular deals like the Francis transfer in the same way they do the £2000 bid they made to little Long Eaton for current England striker Garry Birtles.

"Money is just about the last thing I worry about when I make a signing," says the Forest manager. "The first test is ability. If Peter and I think a player has skill—attacking or defensive—we are always interested.

"So many people in football are scared to back their own judgement. For instance there was a centre-half we heard about playing for Tranmere Rovers many years ago.

"There were reports that about two dozen clubs had spent the season watching him. We went up to see Tranmere play. The centre-half looked a class above everyone else.

"We needed no more proof. We went round to the lad's home in Birkenhead that same night. We talked him into signing for Derby County—the club we were in charge of at the time. We told him he would play for England within a year. His name? Roy McFarland.

"He did play for England within the year and went on to become one of the best defenders we have ever seen. The fee was £25,000.

"Since that day I have lost count of the number of managers from other clubs who have told me they fancied signing Roy. Maybe they did but you can't afford to dither once you've seen a player you fancy."

The Clough-Taylor partnership is famous for such smash-and-grab raids.

Peter Taylor is the man who does the spy job. If he says a player is right, Brian Clough has said he would fork out a million pounds without checking for himself.

A million-pound moment— Trevor Francis signs for Forest as Clough and Taylor look on.

"We can all look at Kevin Keegan playing for England and say what a good player he is," says Brian. "It takes a very special skill to stand on a wet, windy day in a local park and pick out a boy who will go to the top.

"It also takes courage to point your finger and say that is the player who has the ability to play in the First Division. Peter Taylor is the best in the country.

"It's the same when it comes to big transfer deals. Everybody in England believed Trevor Francis was a great player with Birmingham. But they all pulled back when the fee was mentioned. They knew the critics and the public would be up in arms at the thought of somebody paying a million pounds for one player.

"We knew that, too, but we were determined to get the skill of Trevor into our team. If the price was a million pounds then that is what we would pay.

"If a player came on the market at £5 million and we thought he would improve Forest we would try to raise the money.

"Football is big business these days. We also look out on the selling side of the transfer market. In business you try to make a profit so that you can extend and improve your shop.

"If we get a good offer like the £1½ million for Francis then we look on that as half a million profit to spend on other players or to improve the City Ground.

"We also bet that we can spot enough youngsters with talent to

replace any players we sell. What that adds up to is hard work. Every single day Peter and I discuss the transfer market. Buy or sell? Will it be to the benefit of Nottingham Forest and their supporters?

"It's the only way for us. We started with a small club on gates of 12,000. We are now competing with giants like Manchester United, Liverpool, Hamburg, Real Madrid. We have to make our own money. Attract the Nottingham people. With two European Cups in the bag we haven't made a bad start."

MARTIN PETERS
Norwich City

13

RED DEVILS SUIT ME!

WHEN I put pen to paper and signed for Manchester United in the summer of 1979 I was launched into a world that I believe is unique in English football.

The importance of the game to the people of the area has to be seen to be believed. The fans live for football every day of the week.

At my former club, Chelsea, we had a hard core of fanatical fans. But football in London is just a game, not a way of life.

In Manchester, Saturday is match day. The husband sends the wife out shopping and heads for the ground. It is great to be involved with a club that is supported in that way.

We live in a quiet village outside Manchester. But even there we can't really get away from the enthusiasm.

When we lived outside London we used to get kids walking past the house and looking in. In Manchester they come right up to the door, knock, and ask for your autograph.

It makes for more all-round involvement in the game and I have certainly enjoyed that since the transfer.

I had been looking to get away from Chelsea for quite some time before I actually moved. The London side were relegated in my last season and I hadn't enjoyed my football.

It was as much my fault as anyone else's that we went down. Obviously, we didn't play well over the season.

It was becoming more difficult for me each week. It used to be said that our style and methods hinged on me and teams were sending out a man each week with the sole purpose of snuffing me out.

Since the transfer to Old Trafford, however, the pressure has decreased considerably. Opponents can't afford to concentrate solely on marking me. There are so many other good players around who would take advantage.

I have gained a great deal of confidence from playing with international class players throughout the team—and that's no disrespect to the boys at Stamford Bridge.

I moved to Old Trafford to improve my game and also to win cups and championships. I had won very little in my Chelsea days.

I am convinced that my game has come on a lot. I expected it would as I was teaming-up with Dave Sexton, who had been Chelsea manager during my early days at the Bridge.

I knew Dave when I was 16—17 and I had great respect for him as a manager and coach. Part of the appeal of joining United was being re-teamed with Dave.

The other attraction was the ability of the Old Trafford outfit to win things.

We did very well in my first season. The biggest disappointment was being put out of the FA Cup early on by Spurs. We really thought we were capable of lifting that trophy. But that goal by Ossie Ardiles sank our hopes.

But finishing second in the table to Liverpool was still a good achievement. Especially as at the start of the season few people gave us any chance of ending that high in the league.

In fact, we were the only team to stay in the top three all season. That was something we are sure we can build on in the future.

I believe the United side adapted very well to me being in the line-up. Before I arrived they played a different type of game. Full credit must go to the lads for adjusting so well.

We have built our strength on working as a unit. And with another year behind us, logically we will be a better team.

It was very rare at one time for Southerners like myself to leave their own area and move North. Transfers the other way were quite frequent but we tended to stick to home ground.

But more and more players are seeing the appeal these days.

The North of England has a lot to be said for it. Life is lived at a slower pace than in the capital and above all there is passion about the football.

The game consumes the fans' interest day after day. United get terrific crowds coming to Old Trafford. The atmosphere is tremendous.

A player couldn't wish for anywhere better to play.

The goal that dashed United's dream of cup glory.

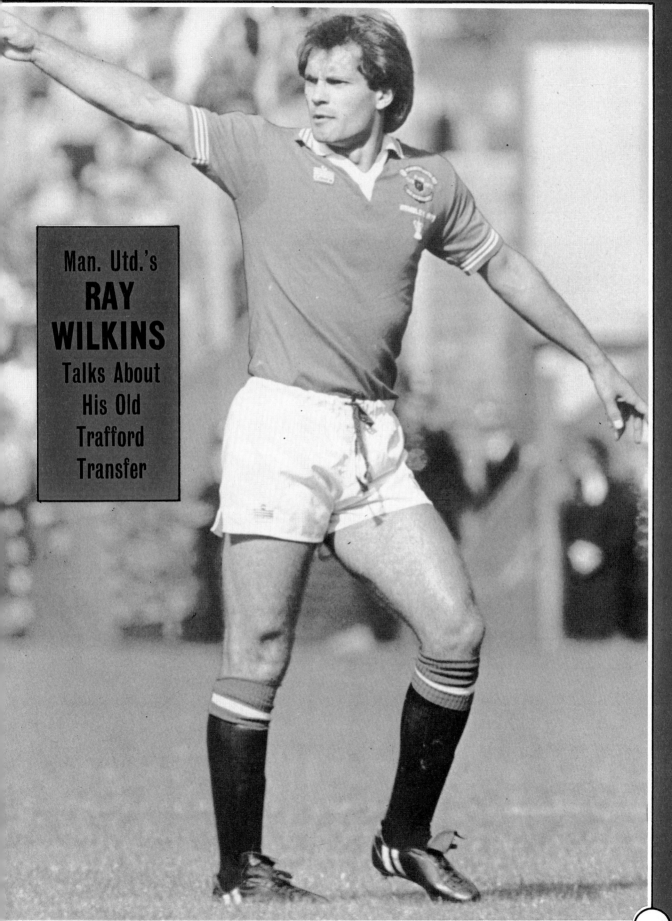

Man. Utd.'s
**RAY
WILKINS**
Talks About
His Old
Trafford
Transfer

16

JOHN WARK
Ipswich Town

PETER SAYER
Brighton

17

B

IT'S A DREAM COME TRUE—

says Manchester City's teenager TOMMY CATON

MOST boys turning out for their school team on Saturday mornings make believe that it's Saturday afternoon and the playing field's one huge stadium with thousands of fans packed into the stands. That the opponents are really top stars like Kenny Dalglish, Ossie Ardiles or Andy Gray. I reckon I'm a very lucky fellow. My dreams came true.

I would play for my school team in Liverpool in the morning. As soon as the final whistle went I would change and be off to play for Manchester City reserves in the afternoon. I was just 15 years old but there I was out on the big First Division grounds face to face with some very famous names.

A year later City coach Malcolm Allison promoted me to the first team. Suddenly I was marking the players whose photographs were plastered all over my bedroom walls. The dream of one schoolboy had come true almost before I had chucked my schoolbag into the dustbin.

I have made my share of mistakes in a season where City struggled. But I can honestly say I have not suffered too badly from nerves.

I had always wanted to be a professional footballer. I was a great Liverpool fan and I knew they were interested in signing me. So were Everton, Manchester United and City. I had a careful look at the centre-half position in all four clubs.

I wanted to see which team might need a centre-half before too long. At the time England centre-back Dave Watson was with City. I knew he was over 30 so I reckoned there might be an opening there before, say, four seasons. I opted

" EVERY GAME'S A BIG ADVENTURE "

for Maine Road thinking I would be doing fine if I made the first team before I was twenty.

I stayed at school until I was 16. Although I was playing for City reserves my headmaster insisted I turn out for the school team.

I was bigger than most but I can tell you schoolboy football was no cakewalk. There are so many players around with real talent but only a very few ever get picked up by the big clubs.

Joining City I had to quickly learn to stand on my own two feet. At first I travelled through to Manchester each day from Liverpool for training. I found that exhausting but I enjoyed the comfort of home in Liverpool with my parents.

Eventually it proved too much. I got so tired I would occasionally miss my train in the mornings and that was costly. A fine for being late is the rule at City.

I moved into digs in Manchester but I didn't have a car. Even when I got into the first team I would have to go and queue for a bus with the fans while the rest of the team jumped into their cars.

It's quite an experience going home on the bus after you have lost. Even the driver chips in with some crack!

HARD TIMES

I couldn't say it was an easy first season. We had a hard time of it but I will always be grateful to Malcolm Allison for keeping faith with me. It would have been so easy for him to blame a 16-year-old but he kept telling me I could make it. I have got to say, too, that very few opposing players tried to take advantage of my inexperience.

Only one forward tried anything on. He charged into me in the penalty-area then took off in a big swallow dive shouting for a penalty. Fortunately the referee had spotted what was happening and waved play on. I had been standing horror struck thinking I had given away a penalty—and we were leading 1-0 with two minutes to go!

The biggest thrill of all was to play against Liverpool at Anfield. Although we lost I felt I had given a reasonable show in front of the crowd I had joined so often on the terraces. Even the Kop chanted my name that night and I was proud to be out on the pitch. I wasn't so enchanted when I stuck the ball in for an own goal right in front of the Kop. They cheered me again!

Now I am hoping to keep making progress with City. I realise how lucky I have been to get so much experience at an age when most professionals are still apprentices. If I don't take advantage it will be my own fault. I will feel I have let down my parents who have given me so much encouragement.

But you can never take anything for granted in life. When I was at school I had planned to become a teacher. I got my O levels. Now I have a tutor who takes me for A level maths. I go back to the ground in the afternoons for the lessons and eventually I hope to qualify as a teacher.

That way I can play my football knowing if the worst happens and I get a serious injury I can fall back on another career.

But for the moment I am seeing stars. Every game is another big adventure. I can only tell the boys who shared my dreams that they must keep battling away. It is easy to be discouraged but if you work hard enough you never know when your chance might arrive. Make sure you are ready to take it.

MALCOLM ALLISON

DAVE WATSON

GLENN HODDLE
Tottenham Hotspur

TOP-NOTCHERS!

Two stars who've helped keep Ipswich Town in the top flight.

Left – goal-grabber PAUL MARINER. Right – up-and-coming defender TERRY BUTCHER.

SANDY JARDINE
Rangers

ANDY KING
Everton

23

JEFF CLARKE
Sunderland

24

GARRY BIRTLES
Nottingham Forest

My Worst Moment

TOP PLAYERS REMEMBER MOMENTS THEY'D RATHER FORGET

JOHN BROWNLIE (Newcastle United) — "My worst moment? That's easy, It lasted all of 90 minutes at Hampden Park in the spring of '72 when I was in the Hibs side that lost 6-1 to Celtic in the final of the Scottish Cup.

"It was my first-ever Cup final, I gave away a couple of the goals and as a side we were about as effective as an umbrella in a hurricane.

"As one wag said afterwards . . . 'We turned up for the occasion, but didn't bother to play. We were only there to make up the numbers!'

"I'll never forget it, hard as I try."

IAN MOORES (Orient) — "Strangely enough my worst moment was a triumph at the time.

"My debut match for Spurs against Middlesbrough in a League Cup tie . . . and I scored the winning goal.

"Followed up by scoring another in the next match as we beat Manchester United 3-2 at Old Trafford.

"The trouble was the Spurs fans expected something special in my first home match.

"Although I did score another to make it three goals in four games I just couldn't keep it up . . . and the fans didn't like it.

"They really got on to me when I didn't score, and I just lost all my confidence.

"In the end I used to really hate playing at Tottenham. I couldn't wait to get away.

"When I joined Orient I scored two goals in my first match . . . and I was really worried the same thing would happen.

"I even wished I had not scored. But when I had a bad run the Orient fans were much kinder to me, and I have enjoyed my stay with the club."

JOHN McALLE (Wolves) — "I must be the only player to break his leg within ten seconds of coming on to the field.

"It happened last year in an F.A. Cup tie against Watford. I was substitute and was sent on with 30 minutes to go to try to shake our lads up a bit. We were drawing 0-0 and struggling.

"I thought the best way would be to make a really telling tackle as early as I could. The opportunity came and I dived in against Watford's Ian Bolton.

"It was the perfect tackle. I could hear the fans saying, 'That's just what we needed,' then I looked at my leg and saw it was swinging loosely just above my ankle.

"I knew it was broken and I was absolutely sick about it because the League Cup final was coming up next month and I knew I would miss it.

"It was the biggest disappointment I've had in my career."

John McAlle with some of the greeting cards he received after his injury.

26

JOHN BURRIDGE (Crystal Palace) — "My worst moment came when I was a teenager playing in the Fourth Division with Workington, a club no longer in the Football League.

"We were hammering Southend United 4-0. A cameraman behind my goal told me we were playing injury time.

"Just then a Workington team-mate hit a back pass to me. As I clutched the ball I heard the referee blow his whistle.

"I turned towards my goal, let out a victorious cheer and blasted the ball into the net as I ran to collect my gloves and cap.

"My team-mates were staggered. The whistle had been blown by a supporter. The ref. had to award a goal. I felt an absolute idiot."

PETER MELLOR (Portsmouth) — "My worst moment was the F.A. Cup Final between Fulham and West Ham Utd. in 1975.

"I was in the Fulham goal and we lost 2-0.

"The 100,000 at Wembley and the millions on TV saw a couple of my mistakes.

"A shot that bounced off my chest and another shot that I dropped.

"Both led to goals for West Ham, and Fulham failed to win the F.A. Cup . . . A match that had been built up by the return of 'old-timers' like Alan Mullery and Bobby Moore, two England men making a return to Wembley.

"Even now it's a game I am seldom allowed to live down but I always make the point that I played my part in helping Fulham reach Wembley."

WILLIE CARR (Wolves) — "No question, it was the night of May 4, 1976. when Liverpool came to Molineux needing a win to lift the First Divison Championship. Wolves desperately needed victory to give us a chance of avoiding relegation.

"Our fans went wild when Steve Kindon scored the first goal for us. But Liverpool came back and eventually won 3-1. As we walked off our supporters tried to cheer us up, but all we could hear were the Liverpool fans singing and roaring away.

"It was worse in the dressing-room. Up the corridor Liverpool were dancing and cheering.

"Down our end it was awful. Nobody could say a word. We just sat there knowing we were down in the Second Division."

ALAN DEVONSHIRE (West Ham) — "I was a youngster with Crystal Palace when Malcolm Allison arrived as manager. Straight away he chopped the playing staff . . . and I was one of the ones to go. I don't think he even saw me play.

"I had set my heart on becoming a footballer. When I got the chop I gave up football for several weeks and took a job in a local factory. In the end my dad almost dragged me along to the non-league club Southall, and I agreed to join them.

"I thought my chances of becoming a professional had gone . . . but then West Ham eventually took a gamble on me.

"It all turned out right in the end. But I shall never forget being told that Palace didn't want me."

WILLIE DONACHIE (Portland Timbers)- "Scoring an own goal against your country in front of your fans has to be one of the most agonising experiences a player can go through.

"It happened to me playing for Scotland at Hampden Park against Wales. We were leading 1-0 with just a minute to go when our 'keeper Jim Blyth threw the ball out to me. I set out to roll the ball quietly back towards him but somehow I miskicked and the ball flew in to the net.

"That cost us victory and with so little time left I could do nothing to make amends. I just wanted to crawl off Hampden. There was nothing I could do or say that would change things. That was two years ago. To this day I can vividly recall every chilling second of that disaster."

GARY OWEN (West Bromwich Albion) — "The £450,000 move that took me to West Brom during the summer of 1979 was the worst moment in my career.

"I had no complaints about the prospect of playing for Albion. But my previous club, Manchester City, meant so much to me.

"I was bitterly disappointed when chief coach Malcolm Allison told me I didn't fit in his plans. When my father drove me to Maine Road for the last time to pick up my kit he said it was like taking a dog to be put down.

"I have no regrets about joining West Brom. But City will always be very special to me."

Two sides of the life of Liverpool's RAY KENNEDY. At home, Ray is a key man in the life of wife, Jennifer and daughter Cara. Away from home, Ray is a key man in Liverpool's title winning team. Here in action against Arsenal with Pat Rice giving chase.

Ray KENNEDY

HOME and AWAY

JIMMY RIMMER
Aston Villa

29

WOLVERHAMPTON WANDERERS striker John Richards has known more highs and lows than most players in the game. They are all plotted in scrapbooks, kept by John and his wife, Pam. Within the pages are cuttings, match programmes, match tickets, England call-up letters and all the treasured souvenirs of an exciting career. Here are a few extracts . . .

April, 1969

RICHARDS A BIG HIT

I score six times for Lancashire Schoolboys against the English Public Schools at a tournament in Bognor. We win 6-0.

The game brings me to the attention of Wolves, who sign me once I've completed my education.

December, 1969

NAP HAND FOR WOLVES STAR

Wolves reserves beat Blackburn 5-3 and I bag the lot.

It's a stepping stone to the first team and I make my debut in March 1970 against West Bromwich Albion at the Hawthorns.

May, 1972

SPURS PIP WOLVES IN ALL-ENGLISH FINAL

My first season in the team after being sub. about 20 times the year before. We reach the final of the UEFA Cup, meeting Tottenham over two legs.

We had beaten the likes of Carl Zeiss, Juventus and Ferencvaros on the way. We hadn't lost any away leg. We even manage to draw at White Hart Lane but they win 2-1 at Molineux to lift the trophy.

June, 1972

UNDER-23 CALL-UP FOR WOLVES STARLET

I'm selected to go on the England Under-23 tour of East Germany, Poland and Russia. I play in all the games and the side finishes unbeaten.

April, 1973

ROCKET RICHARDS BREAKS THE 30-GOAL BARRIER

My first complete season in the side and I net a total of 33 goals. There are a couple of hat-tricks against Stoke and Everton. People start talking of me being "rated in the £100,000 class." At the time, that was some compliment.

May, 1973

SIR ALF GIVES RICHARDS ENGLAND DEBUT

Northern Ireland versus England at Goodison Park and I'm called up by Sir Alf Ramsey as a late replacement for the injured Allan Clarke of Leeds.

It is a superb ending to a terrific season. Wolves had reached the semi-finals of both the League and FA Cup and though defeat was disappointing, the England call makes up for it.

I line up alongside Martin Chivers and Mike Channon. But because we are all central strikers I — as a newcomer — end up on the left wing.

I think I do OK, and reckon it might be the start of a long association with England. It isn't to be.

It's Richards for England —at last!

Wolves striker, John Richards, wins his first England cap against Northern Ireland at Goodison Park tomorrow.

HIGH HOPES AND

30

June, 1973

WOLVES MAN ON TOUR WITH ENGLAND

I'm selected for the summer tour of Poland, Russia and Italy. England are beaten by the Poles in the World Cup qualifying game and the rest of the trip is a terrible let-down for me.

I don't even get on to the pitch and I come home without my second cap. Though I have Under-23, Under-21 and "B" team call-ups in the future, I never have another senior game at international level.

Richards may miss rest of the season

March, 1974

RICHARDS' GOAL IS WEMBLEY WINNER

The League Cup Final and Wolves line up against Manchester City.

I have had to cope with a bad pelvic injury on the run up to Wembley. I'm in agony for most of the game despite the pain-killings sprays.

The score is pegged at 1-1 and the ball is deflected to my feet by City's Rodney Marsh. I let fly and it's our winner.

For the next ten minutes the euphoria of the goal deadened the pain. But I can't say I enjoyed my big day. After that match I'm out for the rest of the season.

HEARTBREAKS—
JOHN RICHARDS' SCRAPBOOK HAS 'EM ALL!

December, 1975

KNEE INJURY FLOORS RICHARDS

An all-too familiar headline in the months to come. I have the first problems with my knee — a twist in training brings up fluid around the joint.

Doctors say there are loose bodies floating in my knee from a previous twist when I was 13. They will have to be removed, but Wolves are deep in relegation trouble and I want to try to help them stay up.

May, 1976

WOLVES DOWN- RICHARDS IN HOSPITAL

I manage 25 goals over the season, but we are still relegated. The day after the season ends I'm in hospital for the removal of my "floating bodies."

I have the whole summer to rest, though, and I'm looking forward to winning promotion next term.

August, 1976

CARTILAGE OP FOR WOLVES STRIKER

Two games into the new season and I collide with our 'keeper in a practice match. The knee goes again. This time I need the cartilage out.

Recovery is swift. Three months later I'm back in the first team.

November, 1976

RICHARDS BACK WITH A BANG

Seven goals in my first four matches back in the side. Things are looking good. We are taking the Second Division by storm.

May, 1977

WOLVES CLINCH CHAMPIONSHIP

We go back to the First as Champions. I've only played just over half a season but I've scored 19 times.

I'm rewarded with a place as an over-age player on England Under-21's tour of Finland and Norway. With David Peach (now Swindon but then Southampton), I'm the old head amongst the youngsters. A great experience.

May, 1978

RICHARDS' SEASON WRECKED BY KNEE TROUBLE

Wolves struggle in first season back in the top flight and again I play on with the knee giving me pain.

It is a routine of playing Saturday, then treatment right up to the next game. I don't train at all. Still, it is worthwhile because we escape relegation.

November, 1978

ANOTHER OP FOR WOLVES STAR

The fluid is affecting my knee again. Doctors give two possible explanations. Natural wear and tear or more floating "bodies."

If it is the first I can't do anything about it. It will finish me as a First Division player. I might even have to pack in football altogether.

Fortunately when I'm opened up they find part of my cartilage has regrown. Trapped against it is more debris. The surgeon whips the lot out and I know I have a great chance of making a comeback.

February, 1979

RICHARDS' GLORY RETURN

Back with a goal again. This time at Arsenal in a 1-0 win. I don't know I'm playing until 2.15. Manager John Barnwell is keeping the pressure off me.

He tells me to park his car in the Highbury car park while the other lads go to get changed. I'm resigned to watching from the stands.

When I get back to the dressing-room Mr Barnwell asks if I fancy playing. I'm in the team from then till the end of the season.

March, 1980

WOLVES LIFT LEAGUE CUP AGAIN

Back to Wembley and after the last time when I had the pelvic trouble, I'm determined to enjoy myself.

We pip holders Nottingham Forest with a goal from £1½ million Andy Gray.

A terrific day out for the players and the fans.

For me it is doubly sweet. After all the time I spent on the treatment table my day at Wembley is pure magic.

IAN WALSH
Crystal Palace

32

ALAN CURTIS
Leeds United

33

BIG FELLAS DON'T SCARE ME!

I HAVE this dream of a skinny, black kid from London's East End running out to play for England in a full international.

And then it fades . . . and in its place there's the same black lad winning the world heavyweight boxing title.

It is only a dream—but I would love either one to come true. And I'm not sure which one I would prefer. Football is my profession and my life just now, but I love boxing just as much as football.

I had to choose between them when I joined Norwich City, and at 16 there was only one real choice—football.

But don't rule out professional boxing in the future for me. I can still see myself as a professional boxer. Boxers don't mature until the middle or late twenties. I've got plenty of time.

I train twice a week with boxers in the evening. I spar, shadow box and do all the moves they do. I don't want to lose touch with boxing.

As a youngster I was a losing finalist in two National Boxing finals as a junior heavyweight. I was on the verge of selection for the England Youth boxing squad—but then I dropped serious boxing for football.

My agent, however, also manages two professional fighters, so I keep very close to the boxing scene.

One thing the sport has taught me. The big fellows are not always the toughest. Sometimes you come across a big fellow who looks frightening in the ring. But hit him once—and he doesn't want to know.

The same applies to some footballers. Big centre-halves can look fearsome, but their bite is often not as bad as their bark. So I'm never intimidated by big defenders.

The other thing that boxing has taught me is to take a knock without losing my temper. In boxing —and in football—the worst thing you can do is lose your head. Get mad at your opponent and he's got you. You have to keep your self-control.

It's harder to control your feelings at football because the knocks you get are often sly ones, or at least unexpected. In boxing you know the other fellow is going to hit you so you're ready for it.

When I have filled out physically I will be a full grown heavyweight, and already my Norwich boss John Bond likes to see me making use of my size in the penalty box.

That has led to a slight disagreement between us. I like to concentrate on footballing skills. I'd much rather try to upset defences by using skill and control. I suppose the answer is a blend of both styles, power and skill. That's what I'm aiming for.

I try to work on my game, practise different skills, after the normal training sessions. And apart from training with the boxers, I like to do some yoga exercises at home. I'm also keen on gymnastics.

I see all these activities as a help to my football. Boxing helps speed, stamina, and footwork. Yoga helps me to relax. It's a mental rather than physical thing. There are tremendous pressures on a youngster in First Division football, particularly one in my position.

Gymnastics helps you to be supple as well as strong. When you have that combination you can try the unexpected—the bicycle kick and things like that which can catch defenders unawares.

"FANTASTIC"

WHEN I was at school I never met a professional footballer. The first time was when I joined Norwich as an apprentice.

Players like Martin Peters, Kevin Keelan and the rest were like superstars to me. It was fantastic, and took me a while to get used to the idea of training and playing alongside them.

I think it's nice to go out and meet youngsters, get them a bit involved with Norwich City, and let them see that professional players are no different from anybody else.

Perhaps that stems from my upbringing. I was born in East London and my parents split up when I was very young.

For a few months my brother John and I were in a Dr Barnardo's home. I can't remember very

JUSTIN FASHANU

much about it now—just small things like playing with pedal cars (I was only four at the time).

After a while at the home my brother and I were fostered by a couple we now call 'Mum and Dad' —Mr and Mrs Jackson. They have been fantastic to us, bringing us up as if we were their own children.

It must have been a brave decision by them in the first place to take on two coloured cockney kids when they lived in a quiet little Norfolk village.

But we were accepted straight away, and being good at sport is always a great help. John is now an apprentice with me at Norwich City, and I have an older brother Philip who plays for non-league Enfield.

I owe a lot to Norwich coach John Sainty. His house overlooks a sports ground, and one day he spotted me playing there in a Norfolk boys match. He invited me to the club for trials, and I was offered an apprenticeship.

John was then youth team manager, and he has helped me all the way through the youth and reserve teams.

Just about everyone at Norwich has helped me at some time, but in particular Ronnie Brooks, chief scout, who has always encouraged me a lot.

When I first got picked for the first team it was a fantastic feeling. We drew 1-1 with West Bromwich Albion, and it was great to be involved.

But I didn't score, which disappointed me. And I didn't score in any of my next four matches in the first team. I began to wonder if I was ever going to hit the back of the net—which is what I was in the team to do.

I needed encouragement then. Particularly from the other lads when I missed the easiest chance of all time in an away match at Leeds.

Norwich City boss — JOHN BOND

Experienced players like Martin Peters and Graham Paddon gee'd me up —and a few minutes later came my breakthrough.

A cross came over and I flung myself at it to score with a diving header. I'll never forget that goal.

Nor the one I scored against Liverpool last season. It was on 'Match of the Day' and won the 'Goal of the Month' award. I hit a swerving volley on the turn that just found the top corner of the net. We lost 3-5 that day to Liverpool, and it was the best match I've ever been involved in.

Being on T.V. that goal 'made' me. Instead of just being known in Norwich I received nationwide exposure.

A few weeks later I was invited to take part in the BBC quiz show 'A Question of Sport'.

There's a funny tale about that. The programme was recorded on a Sunday at the Manchester studios. We happened to be playing Manchester City that week, and I got permission from the club to drive my car instead of going with the other lads on the team coach.

I was supposed to follow the coach—because I didn't know the route too well. But when we got on the motorway I stopped to pick up a hitch-hiker. He wanted to go to Leeds. I said 'Is that on the way to Manchester?', and he said 'Yes'.

So I took him all the way to Leeds before I found out I was about 50 miles out of my way! I finally arrived in Manchester after a journey of about 6 hours. The coach took 3½ hours! The lads gave me some real stick about that.

Getting back to goalscoring I also remember the very first goal I ever scored in schools football. Nothing like my Liverpool effort—it went in off my knee from about one yard range.

But it just shows they all count. They all look the same in the record books.

It would be nice to score spectacular goals every match. But it's not on. I just go out every game hoping to get on the scoresheet.

I hope to do it often enough in the future to establish myself both at Norwich and in the England Under-21 squad. I've had a taster and I loved it.

When I received my cap for playing in the England 'B' match against New Zealand last season it became my proudest possession. It's a beauty and I'd love to have some more.

I want that dream to come true—either part of it.

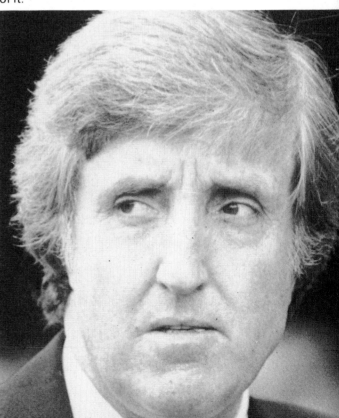

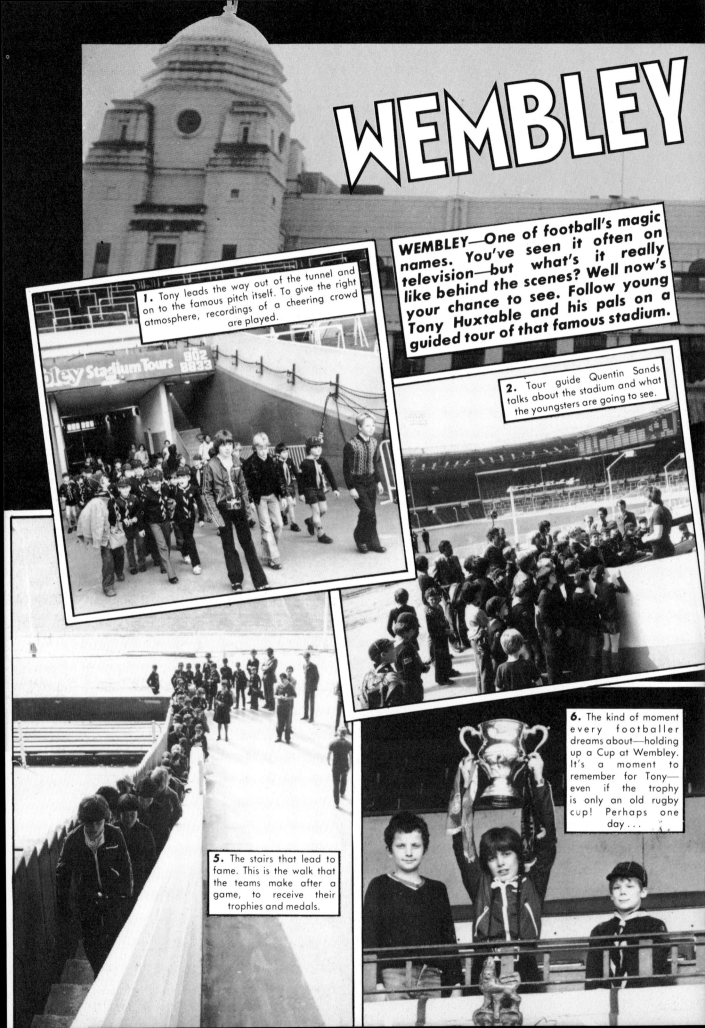

WEMBLEY

WEMBLEY—One of football's magic names. You've seen it often on television—but what's it really like behind the scenes? Well now's your chance to see. Follow young Tony Huxtable and his pals on a guided tour of that famous stadium.

1. Tony leads the way out of the tunnel and on to the famous pitch itself. To give the right atmosphere, recordings of a cheering crowd are played.

2. Tour guide Quentin Sands talks about the stadium and what the youngsters are going to see.

6. The kind of moment every footballer dreams about—holding up a Cup at Wembley. It's a moment to remember for Tony—even if the trophy is only an old rugby cup! Perhaps one day . . .

5. The stairs that lead to fame. This is the walk that the teams make after a game, to receive their trophies and medals.

WALKABOUT

3. This is where the managers and substitutes sit during a big game.

4. Under the stands, the youngsters get an impression of the complicated behind-the-scenes world of Wembley.

7. In the Royal Box—this is where VIPs watch the top matches.

8. Next stop the interview room. Here the party are shown film clips of famous games. One wall is covered with graffiti, and there are terracing-style barriers, so that you can feel really part of the crowd.

9. In the dressing room (a), the guide demonstrates some of the sprays used for treating various knocks. Round the walls are club jerseys.

This is the corner (b), where Bobby Moore always sat on match day. The players' baths and showers (c).

The door that leads from the dressing rooms, into the tunnel—and out to face the crowd (d).

10. The trophy case, containing some of football's most famous honours.

11. Near the end of the tour, and Tony buys a souvenir of his exciting visit.

12. Refreshments in the famous Long Bar. A great way to round off a great day.

Liverpool's
GRAEME SOUNESS
(left) battles for
possession with
West Bromwich Albion's
JOHN WILE

IAN BRITTON
Chelsea

GORDON STRACHAN
Aberdeen

D

MY TWELVE MAGIC MONTHS

Coventry's Up-and-Coming GARY GILLESPIE Takes Stock

IT was a big surprise when at the age of 17 I broke into the Falkirk first team. I made my Scottish Second Division debut on August 20, 1977.

I was absolutely astonished when a year later on August 19, 1978 I made my First Division debut for Coventry City!

I couldn't believe it. There was I achieving my ambition of becoming a professional footballer in England only a year after being given my chance with Falkirk.

I was a part-time player in Scotland, combining turning out for my home town club with a job as a bank clerk.

I found it very hard work being a part-timer. Work at the bank began at 9 am. On some days we would go on until 6 o'clock and I would have to report for training at Falkirk at half past six!

Training wasn't the varied, interesting work we do at Coventry City. As we could only get together about two nights each week we had to cram in all the keep fit stuff. It mainly consisted of running— a real hard slog.

But I enjoyed my football and it paid off when one of the Falkirk regulars was injured and I got my first team chance. I was soon given the captaincy of the side.

It was really only a matter of tossing the coin. I got the job because I was the only one playing consistently at the time and therefore guaranteed my place each week.

I was making good progress at Brockville Park and soon scouts came to see me. Twenty-two games after making my debut, Coventry City asked me down for a trial and signed me on pro forms.

Coventry manager Gordon Milne paid £75,000 for me. At the time Falkirk were around £100,000 in debt. I was proud to think that in a way I had helped keep my home town club in business.

The deal suited all parties. Coventry got their man, Falkirk received their much-needed money and I achieved my ambition.

It was a different world altogther at Highfield Road. The training facilities at our Ryton ground were fabulous and there was I working alongside blokes like Jim Holton and Tommy Hutchison, who I had only seen on television before then.

The man who has probably helped me the most in my time at Highfield Road is former Scotland centre-half Jim Holton. I can't speak too highly of him. He's a great bloke to have around.

On the field he is such a dominating figure. My job alongside him was to pick up anything he missed . . and he didn't miss much.

He had a bit of bad luck in that that he had to drop out of the side to serve suspension. Paul Dyson came into the team and he plays as well and sometimes better than Jim Holton!

DROPPED! BUT I KNEW THE BOSS WAS RIGHT

Playing for Coventry hasn't been without its disappointments. Fifteen games after making my debut I was dropped!

It was a really big blow for me. But I knew Gordon Milne had made the right decision. The reaction of the move up from Scotland had caught up with me. I was mentally and physically tired. I didn't play a full game the rest of the season.

It was then I began to get a little bit homesick. It had been a big upheaval for me and until I had time to think about it it hadn't bothered me. However, when I was out of the side I started to think about the situation.

Trips back home made me realise I shouldn't start feeling sorry because I was out of the team. I would see friends I'd known at Falkirk. They couldn't get a regular game for the club and had become disillusioned.

They would probably have given their right arms to be in my situation!

An even bigger worry was just around the corner for me. In the summer Coventry paid £350,000 for Bristol City's Gary Collier.

He was bought to play in the position I was after. I really worried about my future but I was determined to carry on and fight for my place.

Amazingly Gary was dropped after his debut when we lost 3-2 on the opening day of the season to Stoke City. I was back in the side and after playing only one more game Gary Collier was transferred to Portland Timbers in America!

I didn't feel his departure meant I had won the battle. Actually I felt sorry for Gary. He was a good player and I liked him a lot as a person. He was very unlucky.

However, his ill-luck proved fortunate for me. Eight months after I thought everything was looking black for me at Coventry I was picked to play for the Scotland under-21 side against England at Highfield Road.

It was a great honour to actually play. People thought it was my first call-up. In fact, I had been in under-21 squads in my Falkirk days!

A lot of the players in the squad are almost over age. I hope to become a fixture in the team in the near future.

Looking back on how I played when I was first called up I feel I'm now a lot better equipped to do a good job for Scotland.

The coaches and manager at Coventry have moulded me into a better player. I have become a lot sharper. When I first came down to England I was letting centre-forwards get away with things they shouldn't have done.

The way Coventry play their football has made me a better defender. Gordon Milne always preaches the open attacking style of football.

It puts a lot of pressure on our defence. We can be very vulnerable. But it gives you a lot more responsibility. You know a mistake will be punished. Because we have man to man marking there isn't much cover if you slip up.

If you lose your man there is a great danger you will lose a goal. It has certainly helped me eliminate mistakes.

The fact that I'm not a very quick player has given me the ability to read the game very well.

I have to be aware of moves beginning early or else very fast players will leave me for dead. Reading the game has become one of my big assets.

I feel Gordon Milne is very close to bringing success to Coventry City. He has got together a good bunch of young lads like Andy Blair, Garry Thompson, Paul Dyson and Tom English and linked them with experienced pros like Tommy Hutchison, Mick Coop and Bobby McDonald.

The one thing we have to overcome is the

> Two of Coventry's players of the future —
> *left* TOM ENGLISH, *right* ANDY BLAIR.

tendency to be a Jekyll-and-Hyde outfit. Every pre-season people predict Coventry will pull out some real surprises and beat top teams, but also have some shocking results.

That was never better illustrated than last season. We played Liverpool in the League at home and won 1-0. The newspapers said the Merseysiders were really bad. Fact was we played so well we made Liverpool look bad.

Seven days later we travelled to Third Division Blackburn Rovers and were knocked out of the FA Cup!

If we can overcome that sort of inconsistency I expect to be picking up some silverware to cap the success I've had in my career so far.

DAVID O'LEARY
Arsenal

45

All in the game!

Alianza Lima v. Universitario is the Peruvian equivalent of Liverpool v. Everton. And the authorities there made a mistake when they picked an inexperienced referee to take charge of it.

He was so nervous he blew for the end of the first half when there were still five minutes to go. Realising his mistake in the dressing room he got the players back on to the pitch to play out the remaining period. Then he whistled for half-time. Ten minutes later the teams were back on the pitch for the second half . . . or was it the third?

Definitely a game of three halves.

Amateur referees are often reported being beaten up by disenchanted supporters in South America. But Argentine whistler, Pedro Velez has no fears. He keeps two gorillas as pets and reckons that after going into the cage to feed them, football fans are no problem.

Ponciano Rodriguez has been hitting the headlines in Peru recently. Senor Rodriguez does 90 minutes of exercises before playing for a district team on Sundays. By the way, the gentleman is 80 years old!

Norwegian Fourth Division side Cartherud sold a player to Stavanger IF. The transfer fee—one pound of cheese, four pints of milk, four eggs, one small loaf and a pound of coffee. Must have been a bread and butter player!

What must be one of the oddest bookings of the season happened during a Scottish Junior game between Whitburn and Linlithgow Rose. A Whitburn player was booked for throwing a snowball at a Rose player!

Tom Fairley had been slide-tackled into a snow bank by Jim Harkins. Fairley picked himself up—then threw a snowball at Harkins', thus earning himself a yellow card.

★ ★ ★ ★ ★ ★ ★ ★ ★ ★ ★ ★ ★ ★

We hear a lot about players' lack of discipline in Britain, but in one match in Spain, they had a different problem—the referee beat up one of the players! He was suspended for nine weeks.

★ ★ ★ ★ ★ ★ ★ ★ ★ ★ ★ ★ ★ ★

In an Italy v Switzerland match, Italy had a slight problem with their captains. They began with Dino Zoff as their captain, when he was substituted, Causio took over as skipper. Then he, too, was substituted and Antognoni took over the captain's job!

★ ★ ★ ★ ★ ★ ★ ★ ★ ★ ★ ★ ★ ★

A family affair! During the England v. Eire match at Wembley, Eire's David O'Leary was substituted—and his replacement was his brother Pierce.

St Etienne, the famous French club, reckon they have cut the number of players suffering from colds and flu by 25 per cent. Their method? Installing ten hair dryers in the dressing room so the players don't go home from training with wet hair.

Scottish Premier League match between Kilmarnock and Partick Thistle featured a sensational sending-off. Killie's Bobby Houston came on as substitute—then a minute later was sent off for an off the-ball incident. He hadn't even touched the ball!

An Italian fan has come up with an idea he reckons will produce more skill on the pitch. It's a cubic ball. He believes the bounce will be so unpredictable it will sharpen reflexes and improve ball control!

NO JOKE FOR JIM

The pre-match warm-up at the Coventry v. Norwich turned out to be as sensational as any real game. Coventry's 'keeper JIM BLYTH injured his back during the warm-up, and had to be replaced by third choice 'keeper Steve Murcott who was all set to watch the game from the stand. To add insult to injury Coventry found themselves in trouble for fielding a player who was not on the team sheet given to the ref.

LUCKY!

Sheffield Wednesday's Jimmy Mullen lost a lucky medallion in a pratice game. He has worn the medallion in every match since his apprentice days. Three years later during a match at the ground Jimmy saw saw something bright on the ground—and there was his long lost medallion.

There are some luxury coaches around the First Division these days. It's not uncommon to find dining facilities and TV's on many clubs' transport.

But the new £60,000 vehicle used by AC Milan takes some beating. It has showers, massage tables and even beds to make the journey to and from games just that little bit easier.

Five players were sent off in a recent match in Rosario in Argentina. The teams were made up of league referees!

Santiago Wanderers, bottom of the Chilean League, thought they had found the cause of all their bad results—their playing kit.

So players, directors and manager got together for a special bonfire party—with the shirts, shorts and socks the fuel for the fire.

Next game they turned out in brand new strips . . . and lost again. Maybe they should have burned their boots.

MEL EVES
Wolves

48

GARRY THOMPSON
Coventry City

LARRY MAY
Leicester City

50

TRANMERE ROVERS LEAD THE WORLD

TRANMERE ROVERS live in the shadow of the Merseyside big two, Liverpool and Everton. Making ends meet is a major problem for the Fourth Division side.

But go-ahead Rovers have found the answer—a sports centre which is the envy of many. Included are squash courts and an indoor crown bowling green—the only one of its kind in the world.

On the field Tranmere may not yet measure up to the Merseyside big two—but for off-the-field enterprise they can compete with the best.

IT'S A DERBY DOUBLE

*Action and big names from two matches where rivalry is always red hot –
Manchester United v. Manchester City and Liverpool v. Everton.*

United's STEVE COPPELL faced by City's STEVE DALEY

City's KEVIN REEVES battles with United's ARTHUR ALBISTON.

GORDON McQUEEN, United beats City's DAVE BENNETT in the jump.

City's midfielder PAUL POWER.

United's ace striker JOE JORDAN

Liverpool's playmaker GRAEME SOUNESS

Everton defender JOHN BAILEY

RAY KENNEDY (Liverpool) jumps with Everton's TREVOR ROSS

KENNEDY and ROSS clash again.

ALAN KENNEDY and ALAN HANSEN — join forces to clear the ball.

53

TRAFFIC JAM PUT ME ON

IF it hadn't been for a traffic jam on Wandsworth Bridge on February 27, 1978, I wouldn't be an Aston Villa player now, enjoying the most successful period of my career!

The hold-up signalled the beginning of the end of my spell with Chelsea.

Let me explain . . .

At the time I was an established member of Chelsea's first-team managed by Ken Shellito. It was a rule that players arrived at Stamford Bridge an hour before kick-off on match days.

That night we were due to face Orient in an FA Cup replay. I had always stuck to the club rules and as usual set off in good time to arrive at the ground before the deadline.

Unfortunately there was a build-up of traffic on Wandsworth Bridge and I arrived at Stamford Bridge fifteen minutes late.

It was still 45 minutes before kick-off, but when I walked into the dressing-room Ken Shellito told me I was dropped!

I eventually got back in the team. But the manager kept on chopping and changing the side and I became a bit fed-up. I asked for a transfer.

Villa boss Ron Saunders offered £100,000 for me. I wanted to go to Villa Park, but the deal was put on ice for a spell because Chelsea wanted me to honour my contract.

Finally, Shellito was sacked and Frank Upton became temporary manager. His first job was to sell me. A day later I was an Aston Villa player.

BOMBSHELL

The idea was for me to play up front as a winger with Andy Gray and Brian Little. I'd always been a flankman and was looking forward to the link-up.

I played 25 times up front in my first season at Villa.

It was a bit of a settling-in period, but I did fairly well and that summer I couldn't wait for the new season.

However, pre-season Ron Saunders dropped a bombshell, when before a friendly match against Dutch side F.C. Twente he asked me: "Will you play full-back?"

John Gidman was in dispute with the club and the manager wanted me to take over from him! I must admit at first I dreaded the thought. But I reassured myself that the switch was temporary until 'Giddy' sorted out his problems.

I kicked-off the 1979-80 season in Villa's number two shirt. Gidman came back for a few games and I reverted back to my winger's role.

Then John Gidman was transferred to Everton.

The manager told me if I didn't want to play permanently at right-back he would go into the transfer market and buy someone. But he felt I could do the job for him. He showed so much faith and confidence in me I just had to give it a try.

My first thoughts about taking the place of a former England player were that they were going to be big boots to fill. 'Giddy' was a very popular player with Villa fans.

He couldn't quite accept it when he asked for a

KENNY SWAIN

54

THE RIGHT ROAD — Aston Villa's KENNY SWAIN Tells His Story

move and the fans turned against him. Hero one minute and villain the next.

But that is how supporters are. If you are prepared to give 100 per cent. and are loyal to the club they will love you. I gave them that and in return they gave me support during the switch from winger.

Since the move, the manager has had plenty of chance to buy a full-back. Quite a number have become available on the market. The fact he didn't proved to me he thought I was doing a good enough job.

The seal on the positional switch came when my old club Chelsea visited Birmingham City last season. I went to the game and chatted afterwards to my old teammates.

None of them took the mickey or even mentioned about me moving from the wing. That pleased me no end. Also the fact my move has gone largely unnoticed means to me I have been accepted as a full-back.

I can now honestly say I have never had any real urge to play up front again.

So here I am Kenny Swain playing professional football at right-back.

If you had told me THAT when I was an 18-year-old I would never have believed you. And I don't mean just the fact that I am not a winger any more . . . I never intended playing football professionally either!

At the age of 15 I was rejected by Bolton Wanderers and I was glad!

The life of a football apprentice didn't appeal to me. It wasn't really what I expected. The demands were too great. I didn't like having to travel twice a week to Bolton from my home in Liverpool and every day during the school holidays.

I enjoyed my football and I also enjoyed school. Being rejected by Bolton made it easy for me to decide which to go for.

My school teachers felt it would be a mistake if I made football my career. They thought I would be wasted if I didn't stay on at school. I did continue with my studies

BRIAN LITTLE — Villa goal-snatcher

RON SAUNDERS — Man in charge

and gained eight O levels and two A levels.

It was my teachers' influence that made me decide to go to teacher training college at Shoreditch in Surrey.

I had never been one for leaving home as a youngster. I loved home life. But my three years in Surrey opened my eyes. I learnt a lot and matured.

I played for the college at football. I don't think I have ever enjoyed my game as much as I did then. I was eventually picked to play for the South East Colleges against the South West Colleges at Wycombe Wanderers' ground.

After that match, Wanderers' manager Brian Lee asked me would I like to sign for the Isthmian League outfit. They let me carry on with studies at Shoreditch so at the age of 21 I was playing non-league football.

I had only played for Wycombe about eight times when Brian Lee told me a few Football League teams were interested in signing me up.

Swindon Town, Reading and Oxford United were named . . . then came the shock. London glamour club Chelsea also wanted me!

I got a letter from assistant-manager Dario Gradi inviting me down for pre-season training. Two weeks of the trial had passed when the then Chelsea boss Dave Sexton asked me to sign permanently.

I suddenly realised this was a tremendous opportunity for me. Chelsea were confident I could make it, so I went against all my earlier principles and became a footballer.

I wrote an apologetic letter to the school I was supposed to start teaching at in the August and became a Chelsea player!

My whole life has been a string of contradictions. Not wanting to leave home, so I eventually went away for three years in Surrey. Only wanting to play football for fun, I signed for a First Division outfit. Wanting to make my career as a winger, I decided to move to full-back.

I think now I have finally got everything sorted out. That traffic jam helped put me on the right road.

BOZO JANKOVIC,
Middlesbrough

56

TOTTENHAM TRIO
John Pratt (right) lines up Ossie Ardiles and
Ricardo Villa to face a free kick.

PAUL BRADSHAW
Wolves

TERRY COCHRANE
Middlesbrough

MY first match for Ipswich Town was an away game at Derby. We won 1-0, and it should have been a great moment for me.

But after the game I sat in the dressing room completely bemused—trying to remember how many times I had actually touched the ball during the match.

All I could remember was watching the ball sailing over my head.

From our defenders up to our strikers, from Derby's defence to their attack. The mid-field players were spectators. This was completely strange to me. In Holland I was used to a style in which the ball was played through the mid-field—on the ground.

I couldn't understand why Ipswich had paid £200,000 for me, a huge fee by Dutch standards, just to make up the numbers.

But I shouldn't have been surprised by my first experience of English league football. When I signed for Ipswich my old team-mate at F.C. Twente, Arnold Muhren, who had been at Ipswich since the season's start, told me the style was totally different.

He told me I would find it strange at first.

I certainly did. But I also found it exciting once I got used to it. The crowds are much more involved in the game in England and that atmosphere is transmitted to the players.

In Holland the game is much slower. The play is built up patiently and methodically from the back. It is technically good—but it is often not very interesting for the fans. In Holland crowds are going down all the time. Sometimes only 2000 people watch First Division matches.

The average crowd for F.C. Twente is about 7000. But that's boosted by one or two big crowds for the visit of teams like Ajax, Feyenoord and PSV Eindhoven. The smaller teams attract only two or three thousand spectators. So there is little atmosphere at the matches.

Things are totally different in England. I think the English could learn something from the Dutch, and vice versa. Combining the two styles of play would create exciting and technically good football.

I think that is what we are now doing at Ipswich. Since Arnold and myself settled into the Ipswich team the style has changed. When we joined, the basic style was a long ball up to Paul Mariner or whoever was up front. Arnold and I were not really able to play our best in that kind of set-up.

One day in a team meeting, Bobby Robson, the manager, said " We must give the Dutch boys the balls to create something."

CALL ME SAM!

We began to play more through the mid-field, developing a more accurate style of play, a style of play that in a year or so could make us the best team in England.

There was something else I could not understand when I first arrived at Ipswich. I was introduced to all the players and remembered the names—Kevin Beattie, John Wark, Allan Hunter, Mick Mills, Paul Mariner and so on.

Then in training all I heard were names like 'Bomber', 'Snickle', 'Monster', 'Jaws', 'Big Man' and so on.

Everyone seemed to have a nickname. In Holland everybody is called by their proper name.

Soon I'd picked up a nickname as well. Somebody called me 'MCL' because I look like the television character Marshal Sam McCloud, and this soon became 'Sam'. Now I am 'Sam' to everyone at Portman Road.

Kevin Beattie is 'Monster', Arnold is 'Snickle' (I don't know why), Mick Mills 'Bomber', Allan Hunter is 'Big Man', John Wark is 'Jaws', Alan Brazil 'Pele' and Paul Mariner 'P.M.'.

The atmosphere in the dressing-room is a lot different in England. There is a lot of joking right up to kick-off.

In Holland the players treat the build-up to the match far more seriously. The dressing-room is very quiet, everyone concentrates on getting in the right attitude for the game.

The players go out on the pitch for a thorough warm-up at least 30 minutes before the start. When I start with Ipswich I find it strange to have only five minutes to warm up before the kick-off. But at home matches now most of the players go into our gymnasium for a better warm-up, and this is good.

I feel I am lucky to have come to England at the right time. Playing here has made me a stronger player, and this has helped me to win a place in the Dutch international squad.

There is no doubt the season is harder in England. There are many more matches, and they are all tough. In Holland there are only 34 league games, and one cup competition. The most club games you could play in a season is about 40, unless you do well in Europe, when it could be 50.

In England 50 is about the minimum for a successful side. Some of the clubs play more than 60 matches a season. I was getting tired towards the end of last season, but I enjoyed it.

At Twente I won the Dutch Cup, but that does not mean as much as winning the F.A. Cup. My big ambition with Ipswich is to reach the F.A. Cup final.

I think I have a good chance of achieving it in the next year or two.

Ipswich boss— BOBBY ROBSON

ADRIAN HEATH
Stoke City

62

Lou beats Kenny Burns and Peter Shilton to the ball.

The faces tell the story as the ball misses the goal.

LET-DOWN FOR LOU!

Manchester United's live-wire striker Lou Macari can create danger for any defence.

And even in the air the pint-sized Scot can be a handful — as Nottingham Forest found in this encounter. Unfortunately for Lou his flashing header missed the goal.

Let-down for Lou—relief for Peter Shilton.

ALL-ACTION ARCHIE

Key man in Birmingham City's battle to reach the First Division was non-stop ARCHIE GEMMILL. The camera caught up with Archie on the day of a vital promotion battle against West Ham.

64

In attack or defence Archie is in the thick of the action. (Above) Archie is on hand to put pressure on Ray Stewart and 'keeper Phil Parkes (West Ham). (Left) A heading duel with Billy Bonds.

Archie leads his team off at full-time. It's a no-score draw—but there's been plenty of action. There usually is when Archie Gemmill is around.

ALL SET! Archie prepares to drive to the Birmingham City ground.

Pre-match attention from physio Kevin Walters as he straps up Archie's ankle. Team-mate Kevin Dillon looks on.

Referee and mascot stand by as Archie tosses with rival skipper BILLY BONDS.

IVAN GOLAC
Southampton

66

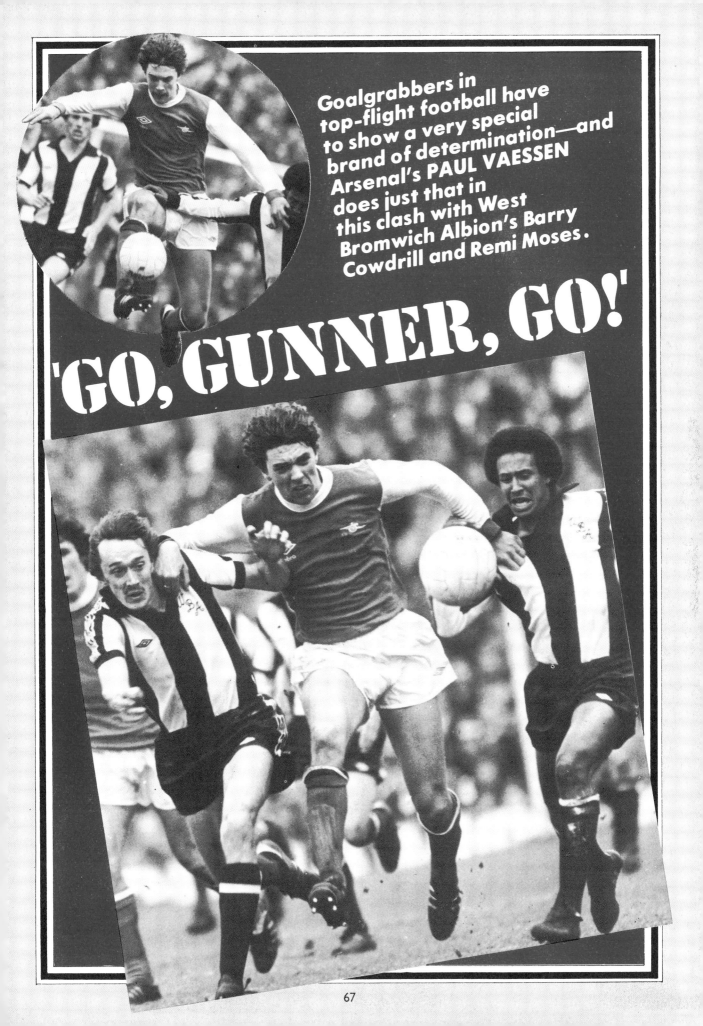

Goalgrabbers in top-flight football have to show a very special brand of determination—and Arsenal's PAUL VAESSEN does just that in this clash with West Bromwich Albion's Barry Cowdrill and Remi Moses.

'GO, GUNNER, GO!'

68

DEREK STATHAM
West Bromwich Albion

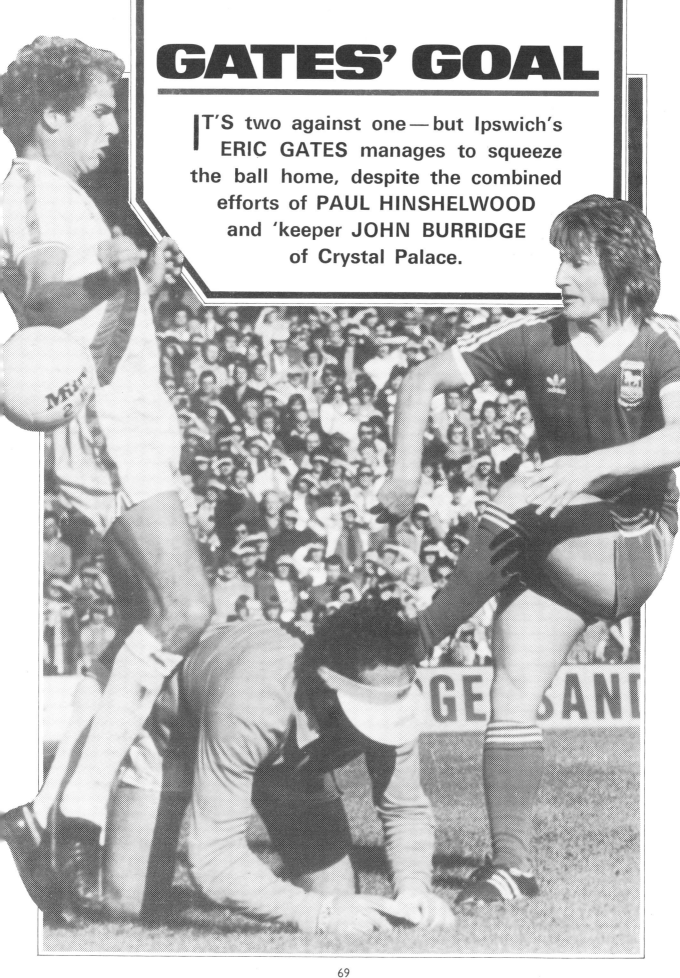

GATES' GOAL

IT'S two against one — but Ipswich's ERIC GATES manages to squeeze the ball home, despite the combined efforts of PAUL HINSHELWOOD and 'keeper JOHN BURRIDGE of Crystal Palace.

IT'S ALL HAPPENED TO ME SAYS EVERTON'S JOHN GIDMAN

I'M A MENACE!

'GIDDY' is the obvious nickname I've had at the three clubs I've played for—Liverpool, Aston Villa and Everton. 'Dennis the Menace' might be more apt!

Unlike Dennis I rarely cause trouble for others—I always seem to get myself in a mess. And to prove my bad luck I have a record of amazing accidents since I was a kid.

One of the worst incidents occured six years ago at a Bonfire Night party. Just established in the Aston Villa team, I was being tipped for England honours, but that Guy Fawkes' bonfire almost wrecked my football career.

A rocket, instead of flying upwards, shot thirty yards across the field and hit me in the eye.

I was rushed to hospital where an eye specialist was called. It was very difficult for the doctors to stop the bleeding and then assess the damage.

I was kept in hospital six weeks, missing three months of the football season. And I was very lucky not to lose the sight in my right eye.

It did go through my mind that I might be finished playing. But the doctors never let me become too depressed. I was soon talking about regaining my first team berth at Villa.

One of my daftest injuries on the football field happened at Ipswich. The ball was fifty yards away as I ran upfield. Unfortunately, I didn't spot a pot-hole in the pitch and slipped into it. Suddenly I was writhing in pain having torn my ankle ligaments and tendons. At first it was thought I had broken my ankle.

The crowd must have been amazed by my antics. It's difficult to sustain a bad injury when you're nowhere near the ball!

The accident that nearly killed me also happened in East Anglia—at Norwich City.

After a Villa match at Carrow Road I decided the dressing-room was too hot. I tried to push a window open but my hand slipped and my fist smashed through the glass.

I was rushed to hospital. My wrist was ripped open and I needed emergency treatment.

The doctor told me that if the wound had been slightly deeper it would have severed an artery. I might easily have died.

But don't think I only try my self-destruct antics in away games.

Once I was kicking a ball around in the Aston Villa dressing-room. The ball hit a fire extinguisher which started pouring foam all over the place.

It was a chaotic scene. After that the Villa players asked me to sit quietly in a corner of the room and not move! They claimed 'Giddy' on the move spells danger.

Perhaps they should have warned my Everton team mates about my past record, because soon after moving to Goodison Park last season I sustained another stupid injury.

This time I was at Bellefield, Everton's training ground. As I was getting changed after a work-out I slipped on a sock and tore a hamstring!

It was very embarrassing for a record £650,000 signing to be sidelined like that.

I've also had long spells out of action with a double cartilage operation. A serious knee ligament injury hampered my progress as well. I was in plaster four weeks.

Then I played in Aston Villa's League Cup victory over my pesent club Everton back in 1977 with a serious groin strain.

Before the kick-off I had three pain-killing jabs. They were so successful I felt nothing until my pelvis snapped.

That injury cost me my England berth and I missed out on a summer tour to Argentina.

My life as a walking disaster area began when I was seven. I tripped over a street kerb and ripped my left eye open. Eighteen stitches were needed to sew up that wound.

A year later I was back in hospital with a broken arm. This time I'd fallen off a slide.

I kept out of trouble for a few years. Apart from having my knee in a splint I was one hundred per cent fit until at thirteen a friend threw me to the ground. The fall cracked my collar bone.

You might think I'm a nervous wreck now. That I must wonder what will happen next.

But if I did worry about the future I'd be grey and haggard. The only thing that does disturb me is that my son Patrick, who is nearly two, might be following in his father's footsteps.

He has a terrible habit of pulling lights off tables and on to himself. I just hope his injury problems ' are a passing phase.

I want to win trophies with Everton and regain my England right-back berth.

Joining Everton was a great move for me. I'm a Scouser born and bred. Liverpool was my first club and I never made the grade there and had to move to Villa to establish myself as a first teamer.

I enjoyed my ten years in the Midlands. But I'm delighted to be back on Merseyside. As well as being my home town I also know all the hospitals in the area—just in case!

AN AMAZING CHAPTER OF ACCIDENTS AND UPSETS, INJURIES AND SETBACKS

ONE THAT GOT AWAY.....

AND ONE THAT DIDN'T!

World class is a label rightly applied to Nottingham Forest 'keeper PETER SHILTON. But even he can be caught out sometimes. As he was by this shot from Ian Walsh of Crystal Palace, which slipped through his legs — and over the line!

PETER SHILTON shows the form that's taken him to the top of the goalkeeping league.

STEVE COPPELL
Manchester United

GREAT DAYS AT THE DELL—

IN the five or six years I've been in the Southampton side no fewer than sixteen full international players have appeared for the Saints, plus quite a few Under-21 or Under-23 caps.

And when I look at the list of men I have played alongside for Southampton I thank my lucky stars for one thing—being born left-footed!

I'm convinced that is the only reason I've managed to keep my place in the Southampton side.

Almost without exception all the best players Southampton have had were naturally right-footed. No matter how hard any player works to become 'two footed' he is always happier on his natural side of the field.

I feel I have made a career out of being left-footed. I have been the one to play on the left and balance out the right-footers.

I have disciplined myself to stay on the left. The only times I pop up on the right are to take inswinging corners—with my left foot, of course.

My main claim to fame is to have played alongside Peter Osgood, Alan Ball, Phil Boyer, Charlie George, Mike Channon, Terry Paine, Dave Watson all of England, Peter Rodrigues (Wales), Ted MacDougall and Jim McCalliog (Scotland), Chris Nicholl (Northern Ireland) and the Yugoslavs Ivan Golac and Ivan Katalinic. Plus Austin Hayes (Eire).

And that's leaving until last the most famous of the lot—Kevin Keegan. What a thrill to play with the best footballer in Europe. I'll never forget the day I learned he was to be joining Southampton.

All the lads had the day off at The Dell. As usual I went off to play squash. I was in the middle of a hectic game when an onlooker called out from the gallery. "Did you know Southampton have just signed Kevin Keegan?"

I thought it was somebody trying to put me off with a joke! Told them to stop messing about and let me concentrate on more serious matters.

When I came off court I heard the news confirmed on the radio—and I had to go and apologise. That was typical Lawrie McMenemy style, producing Kevin at a Press conference like a rabbit out of a hat. Nobody at The Dell knew a thing about it. It was as big a shock to skipper Alan Ball as everybody else.

The boss has a flair for the transfer market. And often the cheapest signings have proved the best.

Peter Rodrigues was signed on a free transfer, and went on to captain the '76 F.A. Cup winning side. Alan Ball, an absolute 'snip' at £60,000, played a huge part in getting us back into the First Division, and establishing our place.

Almost all of Southampton's big name players have been 'characters'. Jokers off the field almost every one. As a quiet man myself I just sat back in the dressing room and enjoyed the wisecracks. I'm sure half our players could have earned a living on the stage.

Ted MacDougall, for instance. What a comedian he could be—in his good moods. Ted was a fascinating character. If things were going well he was as happy as a sand-boy. If they weren't—well, watch out.

On the field Ted was deadly given the right service. There was no ceremony about Ted MacDougall's goalscoring. A poke here, a prod there, a nod of the head, the ball always found its way into the net.

A complete contrast to another Southampton superstar, Mike Channon. Mike has scored some great goals for the Saints —but hardly a single one from inside the six-yard box.

If Mike had been able to finish like Ted MacDougall he'd have topped forty goals a season. I've never seen a player of top class miss so many open goals! Yet Mike laid on many more for others—none more than in the season he played alongside MacDougall. Ted was never the same player after Mike left to join Manchester City.

For all-round talent Peter Osgood was almost the perfect footballer. His skill with the ball

A moment to remember! Kevin Keegan signs for Southampton. Standing (l. to r.) — Steve Williams, Chris Nicholl, Kevin and Dave Watson. Seated (l. to r.) — Lawrie McMenemy and Alan Ball.

SAYS SOUTHAMPTON'S NICK HOLMES

was unbelievable. He put the ball into the most unexpected places with a first-time flick that completely opened up a defence.

Ossie was a smashing bloke. So easy to get on with. If you ever wanted anything you went to see Ossie. One or two of the lads once wanted to buy a greyhound to race. I mentioned it to Ossie. About two days later it was all set up. Ossie had got us a dog, registered it, found a trainer—the whole works.

Ossie, Alan Ball and Mike Channon, amongst others, have all been great fans of horse racing. On days off you always knew where to find them.

Mike's tips have not improved since his stay with Manchester City. He didn't lose the knack of picking losers. Ballie was another shocking tipster.

One time we had a Christmas party at The Dell when everybody received a 'daft' present. We bought Ballie a rocking horse—we reckoned it was the nearest he'd ever get to a winner!

On the field, of course, Ballie was an inspiration. Always doing the simple thing quickly, and always wanting to win.

Possibly he made as big a contribution off the field as on it. Or rather on the training ground. Ballie felt what you put into training showed on Saturday.

His mental approach to the game was superb. Ballie taught everyone that concentration is the most vital thing in football.

THE BIG MAN

I'VE been lucky in growing up at The Dell with the right habits taught to me.

But I've also been helped by my childhood hobby—chess. Between the ages of eight and fourteen I played more chess than football. At the age of twelve I was runner-up in the All England schools tournament.

That means nothing now, and I very rarely play. But playing that much chess taught me how to concentrate. I learned how to shut my mind to all other thoughts.

It's helped me get the mental discipline at football to play alongside more skilful players.

There have been plenty of those at The Dell in my time. Lawrie McMenemy goes for class players when he makes a signing.

But none of the personalities on the playing side at The Dell have overshadowed 'the big man'—Lawrie McMenemy.

He's a big man in every sense—and the lads are never slow to remind him.

We can be on a coach or a train anywhere and if anything larger than life appears it's always 'Lawrie's'.

The year we played in the European Cup Winners' Cup we met Marseilles in France. During a coach trip through France I can remember two good examples.

We went past a superb golfing complex, which was advertised by a gigantic golf ball by the main entrance. 'Lawrie's ball' said Ossie quick as a flash.

A little further on we passed three trees standing very straight next to each other. "Lawrie's cricket stumps" said somebody. It was almost a contest.

Lawrie has big ideas and big ambitions for Southampton. The signing of Kevin Keegan was just a step along the road. It's great to be part of it—thanks to my left foot.

Mr Greenfingers!

For skilful wing play Dave Thomas of Wolves is highly rated. But Dave is due just as much praise for his skill off the field — as a gardener.

Trees flourish, flowers blossom and grass grows green and lush under Dave's care, as a quick look round the Thomas garden shows.

Looks like Dave's nimble footwork on the football field is matched by his green fingers off it.

JOE GALLAGHER
Birmingham City

77

"TALKING & TACKLING –

THAT'S MY GAME!"–
says Spurs' TERRY YORATH

IF I was forced to give up football tomorrow I would still have had a marvellous career.

I've passed 30, the age when people expect you to be thinking of quitting. But I just hope it doesn't all end yet. My contract at Spurs expires in July '82, I wish it was longer.

I'm enjoying my football perhaps more than I have ever done. And Spurs can provide a great climax to my career with some of the medals I've missed out on.

During 11 years with Leeds all I ever won was one League Championship medal, plus a couple of losers' final medals.

I was often in the squad at Elland Road without being in the side.

In my time there Leeds won the League Championship twice, the F.A. Cup once, the Football League Cup once and the UEFA Cup twice.

But I played in only one championship - winning side.

There were so many near misses for Leeds. Runners-up four times in the First Division. Losing finalists twice in the F.A. Cup. Losing finalists in the European Cup, Cup Winners' Cup and Fairs Cup.

I've no regrets of course, looking back at my career. O.K. there were disappointments at Leeds, but it was a great team to be in.

Now at Spurs I'm in a side with the potential to be as good—or even better.

There was one flaw at Leeds and I believe it cost us a lot more success.

Don Revie was 85% a fantastic manager. But when I look back at the number of big games in which we ' froze ' it raises an element of doubt.

Don was so thorough. Every little detail was attended to. The players could not have been better looked after, nor their families.

But somehow all the dossiers and the planning introduced an element of fear.

Instead of having our confidence built up we went into the big matches with niggling doubts.

The result was that we lost a lot of them—to Chelsea and Sunderland in the F.A. Cup, to A.C. Milan in the Cup Winners' Cup, plus some semi-finals and other key matches along the way.

It's difficult to fault Don Revie in anything he did. But something wasn't quite right, or we'd have ended with nearly every honour in the game.

Mind you, we did have our share

DON REVIE'S SECRET WEAPON

of successes and happier times. There was always plenty of fun in the Leeds party. In fact that was one of Don Revie's secret weapons.

We took along our own joker on every trip, to each match!

His name was Herbert Warner, and his job was to keep the jokes going and relax the players before the match.

Herbert never left the dressing-room before a match until 15 minutes before kick-off.

A friend of Don's, he would do anything for Leeds—and almost anything for a laugh.

He wore a toupee and had a glass eye. I can remember on one trip Billy Bremner and Allan Clarke crept into his room and pinched them both so that Herbert couldn't come down to breakfast!

He didn't mind as long as the lads had some fun.

There was also one moment in Turkey I will never forget.

Out there it's the custom for teams to swap subs'

THAT LONG, LONG WALK I'LL NEVER FORGET!

and trainers' benches for the second half of a match.

After half-time in a European match, trainer Les Cocker plonked himself down on the trainers' bench we had used in the first half.

Next moment a Turkish policeman was waving a gun in Les's face trying to move him. But Les would have none of it. No policeman was going to order him off his bench!

Les just sat there defiantly, while the policeman became more and more agitated. When he cocked the trigger of his gun Don Revie hastily persuaded Les it might be a good idea to change benches after all!

Les Cocker was the perfect partner for Don Revie. While Don did all the background planning, Les got on with the training.

He was a great number two because he was no 'yes' man. I've seen Les and Don having a real slanging match in the dug-out during games, but it never lasted because of their respect for each other.

There was a remarkable spirit at Leeds, but it was never quite the same after Don Revie left to take the England job. Even though we managed to reach the European Cup Final under Jimmy Armfield's control.

The final in Paris had bitter memories for me. I was in the team—but on the losing side.

And my main memory of the match is of being substituted in the second half.

We were a goal down, and forward Eddie Gray took my place. That walk off the pitch to the bench was the longest I've ever taken.

After that the team began to break up. I felt it was time for me to go, I was happy to move on to Coventry.

In three seasons there I had some good times, but the club did not quite fulfil its potential on the pitch. Although most clubs in the league could learn a lesson from the kind of facilities for players and fans that Coventry provide.

Last year I could have joined several clubs, including going back to my home town of Cardiff as player-manager.

But Spurs offered me the chance to reach the top again.

I feel we play more entertaining football than the great Leeds side, but with less consistency. That's something we have to work on.

At Spurs I can concentrate on what I do best—talking and tackling.

I can help organise the side, win the ball and then give it to the more skilful players.

It's giving me the most enjoyable period of my career. Some of the skills of young players like Chris Hughton and Paul Miller are breathtaking.

On the international scene I'm lucky to have played so many matches for Wales. I've passed the 50 cap mark, and I'm looking forward to the remaining World Cup qualifying games.

Wales are much more respected at international level these days, thanks to Mike Smith's efforts.

It was a disappointment to the Welsh players when he quit to take over at Hull City. Mike had done so much to raise the standards in Wales.

Speaking of Wales brings me to my childhood in Cardiff and an experience that has remained in my memory ever since.

As a youngster I enjoyed football and rugby, but at my grammar school from the age of 11 we played only rugby. I earned a trial with the Cardiff Rugby Club.

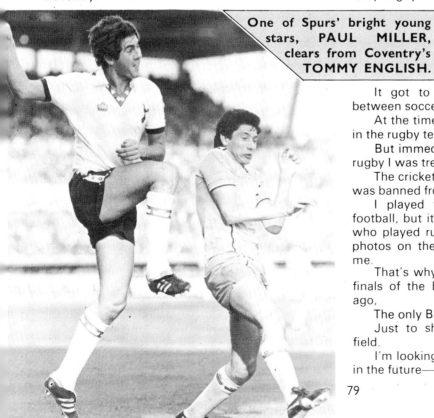

One of Spurs' bright young stars, PAUL MILLER, clears from Coventry's TOMMY ENGLISH.

But outside school I was a keen football player. And my older brother David was good enough to have trials with Arsenal, and to sign for Crystal Palace.

It got to the point where I had to choose between soccer or rugby. I chose soccer.

At the time I was the school cricket captain, and in the rugby team.

But immediately I chose to play football and not rugby I was treated like an outcast.

The cricket captaincy was taken away from me. I was banned from playing any rugby at school.

I played for the Welsh Schoolboys side at football, but it never got a mention at school. Boys who played rugby for Wales Schoolboys had their photos on the wall. It left a lasting impression on me.

That's why it was so good to reach the quarter-finals of the European Championship a few years ago,

The only British side to qualify.

Just to show that Wales is not only a rugby field.

I'm looking forward to more success with Wales in the future—and with Spurs.

SPEED MERCHANTS

On the field, John Connolly, Newcastle United and Irving Nattrass of Middlesbrough show a good turn of speed. Off the field too, they keep up their interest in speed—John with his greyhounds, Irving with his horse.

STEVE EMERY
Derby County

82

KEITH BERTSCHIN
Birmingham City

83

KEVIN KEEGAN
Southampton and England

84

85

STRESS

VIV ANDERSON
(Nottingham Forest)

Big-time football is a
high-pressure game—
as these faces show!

PETER WELLS (Southampton)

JIMMY RIMMER (Aston Villa)

86

AND STRAIN

STEVE DALEY (Manchester City)

IAN GREAVES
(ex-Bolton Wanderers
manager)

BRIAN GREENHOFF (Leeds United)

GORDON McQUEEN, Manchester United

TREVOR
FRANCIS
(Nottingham
Forest)

TONY CURRIE
Queen's Park Rangers

JOHN ROBERTSON
Nottingham Forest

TREASURE SEEKER -

He looks for hidden gems in football's highways and byways.

THE football scout arrived home from his Saturday afternoon expedition—and his wife laughed and laughed when she saw him at the door.

Not because he was rain-soaked, dripping and bedraggled, but because he looked so ridiculous in a coat of tent-like proportions, a soft hat that had seen better days and a giant scarf wound round his neck.

"You can laugh," he grinned to his missus. "I've had SOME day!"

Then came the story of how the game he had watched was out in the country, on a pitch without a vestige of shelter. And it had rained and rained . . .

"A friend offered me a change of clothing," he added. "This is it."

This weather-beaten scout was Jimmy Scott, the Scot from Dundee who is such a successful spotter with Preston North End.

And Jimmy can tell many a story of hard and hazardous times in the search for football gems. For he's been doing it for 34 years now.

The presentation watch he wears carries an inscription telling of 25 years with Preston. But, before that, there were eight years in which he made his mark with Burnley.

There is no room on the watch to name all the big money players Jimmy Scott has sent to Turf Moor and Deepdale.

Archie Gemmill, Alex Bruce, Mel Holden, Jim Blyth, Mike Robinson, Adam Blacklaw, Bobby Seith, Michael Baxter—and so many others down the years.

As well as being weighed up again and again against various types of opposition and in contrasting ground conditions, each Scott prospect is subjected to searching investigations of behaviour and family background and circumstances.

Thoroughness is the watchword.

The scout's report form you see here is only the first of a batch submitted by Jimmy Scott five years ago after being tipped off about a 15-year-old called Mike Robinson, who played for a minor Blackpool team called Dolphinholme.

Mike Robinson, of course, is the fellow Manchester City paid £750,000 for last year. It was Preston's biggest-ever transfer haul.

PRESTON NORTH END F.C.

REPORT No:
FOR OFFICE USE ONLY

Match: *Barnham v Dolphinholme*
Player: *Michael Robinson*   Date: *6th May '74*
Age: *15¾ yrs* Height: *5' 10½"* Club: *Dolphinholme*
Character: *Good Type and Family Background* Weight: *11 Stone* Position: *C-For*
Married or Single: *Single*
Previous Clubs: Am or Pro: *Amateur*
Special Remarks:

REPORT

By: *J. P. Scott*
Movement: *Good* Number of Times Seen: *Once*

Intelligent or Not: *Yes*

Ball Control: *For Build and experience — promising.*

Positional Play: *Grafted and worked forward line from central position well.*

Right Foot: *His natural good-shooting ability*

Left Foot: *Fairish*

Heading: *Obvious ability to work and improve on*

Shooting or Tackling: *Connects and hits good R/F ball*

Forceful or Not: *Promisingly busy, with good zest and drive*

Recommendations: *Arranging to have into Deepdale. For his age has fine stature and a very good balanced movement Particularly impressed me by his natural ability & desire to do strong direct power running on the ball from deep positions with strength and stature to be effective.*

(General Remarks Overleaf)

Distance is no object to this dedicated searcher after football talent. His car's speedometer shows 35,000-40,000 miles for a year's running. He is one of British Rail's best customers. The airways' people also know him well.

Not so long ago he was over in Holland, combing the lesser Dutch leagues following information received. The net is being spread wider these days.

In Thurso and Wick, football outposts in the far north of Scotland, players have also come under inspection by Jimmy Scott.

Often, too, there are tips to off-the-beaten-track spots in Ireland—both north and south.

Says scout Scott, " It's amazing how often Irish boys write in saying they have what it takes for English senior football, and how we should come and have a look at them. Occasionally we do."

KEY MAN

FROM territory much further afield came the prospects who gave a big surprise to residents in a Preston hotel—and to Jimmy Scott, too.

The North End people, acting on their scout's report, decided to bring a coloured player to this country for trials.

He was quartered in one of Preston's best hotels, and came the day Jimmy Scott handed him agreed weekly expenses.

With a whoop of joy he grabbed the money, dashed off down the corridor, through startled residents in the lounge, and out into the street.

Jimmy Scott got to the main door to see his man disappearing into a big store on the other side of the street.

" Money to spend," grinned the fellow when Jimmy caught him up at a counter, already trying to make himself understood to a salesgirl.

And Jimmy stuck around to lend a hand . .

The capture who rebounded, to the considerable gain of PNE, was goalgrabbing Alex Bruce.

A junior from Jimmy Scott's home beat in Dundee, Alec was so keen to join Preston he gave up his chance of a schoolboy international cap to sign.

He did so well at Deepdale, Newcastle United paid £120,000 for him.

But Bruce failed to hit it off on Tyneside, and, a year or so later, he was back with Preston.

Newcastle, in dire need of a centre-half, took a fancy to the Preston No. 5, John Bird.

They offered Bruce in exchange, and the deal was eventually sealed—with £50,000 going to North End as part of the deal.

It was a paying transaction for the Deepdale club . . .

Bruce is again going great guns there, attracting attention from higher-up clubs.

And how do you become a football scout? Jimmy Scott will tell you—

" I was working as a locksmith in Dundee and turning out for a junior football club called Osborne. Came an injury that made me give up playing.

" But I wanted to continue association with the game. When Burnley advertised for a scout in Scotland I had a go. It has all worked out."

Jimmy the one-time locksmith has certainly been a key man for Preston.

ANDY GRAY

ANDY GRAY

Scout Maurice Friel tells the story

WHEN Andy Gray moved from Aston Villa to Wolves last year he broke the one and a half million pound transfer barrier.

Yet the man who gave Andy his first chance in senior football, Dundee United's manager Jim McLean, had to be talked into signing Andy! Only the perseverance of scout Maurice Friel finally convinced Jim. And no wonder Maurice stuck to his guns, for he had been keeping tabs on Andy Gray since he was nine years old.

Maurice had been at one time physiotherapist to Clydebank, the club for whom Andy's eldest brother James played. James would often bring down his baby brother to watch the 'Bankies.

When Andy began to attract attention through his displays at Kingsbridge Secondary School and for an amateur side called Clydebank Strollers, Maurice Friel already knew all there was to know about him.

But his job of convincing Dundee United was made all the harder because Andy had a disastrous trial match at Tannadice.

As Andy himself says—" I had gone there with my brother William who I always turned to for help and advice. But it was a bleak night and I had only finished school in Glasgow a few hours before. Therefore I never played anything like my best."

Maurice Friel, however, knew Jim McLean had witnessed nothing like the real Andy Gray and told him so—repeatedly.

Andy goes on—" In the end I was invited back and this time passed my test with flying colours. As soon as I left school I joined up as a full-timer with United. I was in the first team very soon afterwards. And it's all due to Maurice Friel."

Maurice no longer works for Jim McLean. His full-time job took him to London where he now lives.

But as one of football's treasure seekers he certainly showed he had an eye for a real find!

MIKE WALSH
Bolton Wanderers

92

STUART'S STUNNER!

F.A. Cup semi-finals are often tenser than the final itself so a goalscorer in a semi has plenty to celebrate—as you can see in these pics of West Ham's Stuart Pearson who notched a vital goal in the semi-final against Everton.

In goes the goal.

And Stuart makes sure the camera captures his jubilation.

DOG KENNEL SWUNG DEAL

— ODD STORIES FROM THE TRANSFER SCENE

MILLIONS of pounds, dollars, Deutschmarks and pesetas have passed through the hands of British football clubs in the past year in the transfer market.

Most are pretty straightforward transactions. A manager offering a sum of money to another manager. A case of "you pays your money, you gets your player."

But down the years there have been transfers that were just a little bit out of the ordinary.

Like the one that took Tommy Martin from Doncaster Rovers to Nottingham Forest 17 years ago. There was a bit of haggling over terms when Forest took Martin to look over a house.

"I like the house," he said. "It has a big garden and I have a big dog. If the club will build me a dog kennel in the garden I'll sign."

Forest agreed—and Tommy signed on the dotted line.

In Manchester City's signing of Kaziu Deyna from the Polish club Warsaw Legia, it was the currency which was unusual—or at least part of it.

Warsaw wanted £100,000 for Deyna. But only £70,000 was to be paid in cash. The rest was in the form of medical equipment, which was apparently in short supply in Poland.

The £30,000 Lincoln City paid for West Ham goalkeeper Peter Grotier was also a bit special. It had been raised by the fans at Sincil Bank. The club itself didn't have enough cash to meet the Londoners' requirement.

Grotier, on loan to Lincoln, impressed the home fans so much they were happy to dig into their pockets to secure his permanent transfer.

When Joe Baker moved from Hibernian to Turin in Italy in 1961 he spelt out terms which made this move an unusual one.

Joe demanded Turin also sign his cousin Hugo Blair—who was a bricklayer. Joe didn't want to land in a foreign country without a pal to talk to. The Italians gave Hugo a well-paid job in the club president's office.

Brian Clough is a man rarely out of the transfer headlines. When he was manager of Derby County he was involved in a race with Everton boss Harry Catterick for the signature of Archie Gemmill.

Cloughie arrived at Gemmill's home one evening and after a few hours talking with Archie decided to kip down on the couch whilst the Gemmills slept on the decision.

Archie got up to find Clough washing the dishes and decided then and there to sign for Derby. Brian's all-night vigil paid off because as he was leaving the house Harry Catterick was coming up the street to try to persuade Gemmill to join Everton.

In selling players, too, Clough doesn't worry about straying from the normal.

He bought Asa Hartford for Nottingham Forest for £500,000, then after just three games he agreed to sell the player to Everton.

A meeting was arranged at the hotel where Forest were making pre-match preparations for a League Cup tie with Blackburn. Hartford had entered the hotel thinking he was in the Forest side that night. He left with Everton manager Gordon Lee having agreed to become a Goodison Park player. But that wasn't the end of Asa's adventures. The first match he played for Everton turned out to be a bit of an embarrassment.

Asa drove to Liverpool for the game. He looked up and saw the floodlights, and used them as a guide. When he arrived at the ground and started to park his car he saw a lot of red and white, and realised that he was at Anfield, home of Everton's arch rivals, Liverpool. Then he saw a youngster wearing the blue and white of Everton.

"Know the way to Goodison?" asked Asa Hartford.

"Yes!" said the youngster.

"Hop in," said Asa, "and show me!"

And he arrived in time for the kick-off!

Cloughie has had his failures, too. In 1972 he thought he had the transfer of Nottingham Forest's Ian Moore all sewn up. Moore was even introduced to the Derby fans before a game as the club's new player. He put his signature to paper on the Baseball Ground pitch.

But a technicality made the signing forms incomplete and Manchester United nipped in that night to secure the player right from under Clough's nose.

It all goes to show it's not just the amount of money involved which can make a transfer hit the headlines.

ASA HARTFORD

ON THE SLIDE!

MICK MILLS, Ipswich, hits the deck in a bid to halt Spurs' STEVE PERRYMAN

95

VINCE HILAIRE
Crystal Palace

ALAN YOUNG
Leicester City

97

PUZZLE SPOT

CROSSWORD

LETTER LINKS

Move across, down or diagonally to spot the names of 10 international footballers.

H	A	V	O	R	P	E	H	D	G	N	I
O	T	R	A	N	Y	R	C	R	L	K	O
R	F	N	I	N	R	E	D	A	T	O	B
C	D	N	E	G	K	N	F	H	C	R	S
P	O	J	L	S	O	S	N	Y	L	K	N
P	E	L	T	H	M	A	E	D	W	I	I

TEAM TWISTERS.

Rearrange the letters to form the names of five football clubs.

1—AACEGHIILNTTW
2—DEEHNNNOOPRRSTT
3—BEILOORRRSSTV
4—ADEEHILLNOOPRTTU
5—BDDEGHILMORSU

PICK A LETTER

From the clues below pick the last letter from each of the answers to form the name of a well-known international footballer.

1. A football Moor ----
2. Might be described as one -------
3. Manchester City Pole -----
4. Scotland defender -------
5. The team No. 4 plays for ------
6. Small Manchester United man ------
7. Forest's Garry -------

ACROSS

★★★★★★★★★

7. They play at Gresty Road (5)
8. Queen's Park or Glasgow (7)
9. A studious team? (7)
10. Open them for Eric of Ipswich! (5)
12. Nickname for Aberdeen and Wimbledon (4)
14. A forest Scot (5)
17. Home park for Blackburn (5)
18. Football commentator (4)
21. Glasgow Celtic player with a famous boxing namesake (5)
23. Bad defeat (7)
25. Ran sale to get this club (7)
26. Held in high esteem (5)

4. John served Middlesbrough long and well (6)
5. Obstacle for the upset horses! (4)
6. East Londoners (4,3)
11. Special selections scattered in the cup draw (4)
12. United's Trafford (3)
14. Sheffield Wednesday's favourite bird? (3)
15. Ding dong place for Southampton (4)
16. Liverpool and Scotland player (7)
18. Glenn of Spurs (6)
19. Great English rivals (5)
20. Elland Roaders (5)
22. Roger helped England win the World Cup (4)
24. They have a gig at Gigg Lane (4)

DOWN

1. Net twenty times? (5)
2. Might be lamed winning one! (5)
3. Penultimate stage to the final (4)

PYRAMID CLUBS

1—Clemence to his pals.
2—Billy the Hammer.
3—They called them the magical Magyars.
4—Leicester striker Martin.
5 Scottish football club.
6—Where Orient are at home.

		R	
1	A		
2	N		
3	G		
4	E		
5	R		
6	S		

PICK A TEAM.

Choose the players from the clues given alongside—

1. _____ Place a Fulham man from old TV series.
2. _____ A gunner's staple diet.
3. _____ Palace thunderball.
4. _____ Does he sing The Desert Song at Anfield?
5. _____ Ready to bat for Norwich.
6. _____ " Old Man's Sport " with Forest.
7. _____ No chip on it at Newcastle.
8. _____ Ipswich's South American.
9. _____ Does he cross the river for United?
10. _____ Mobile Wolves man.
11. _____ Spurs house holder.

Answers on page 116

DAVID GEDDIS
Aston Villa

99

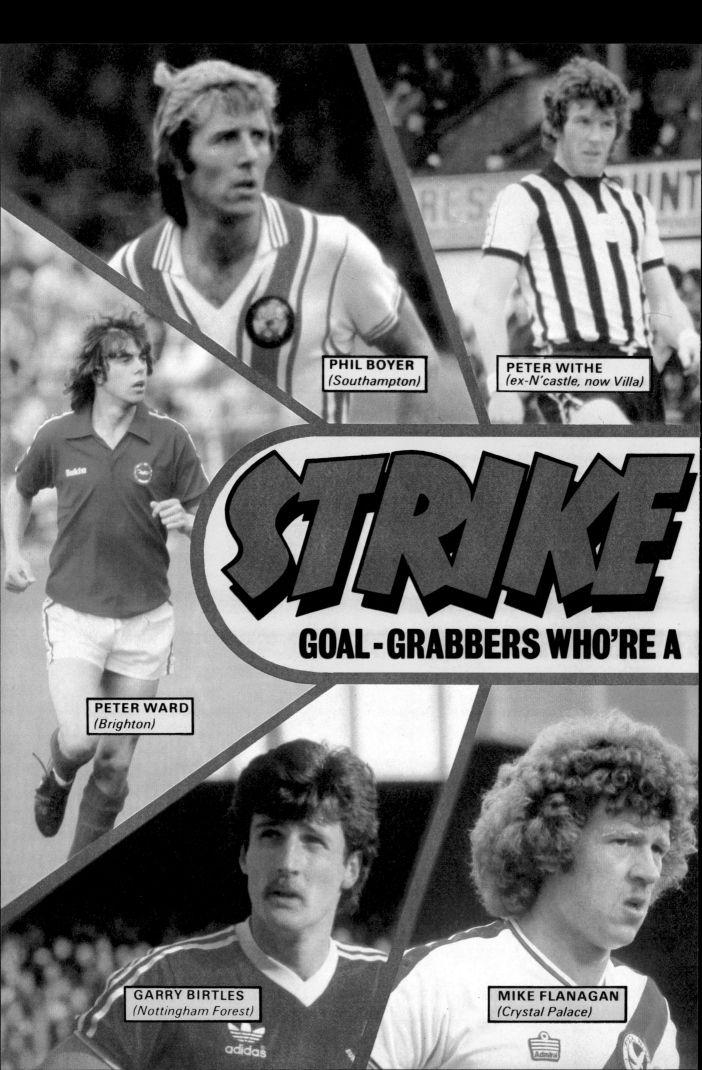

PHIL BOYER
(Southampton)

PETER WITHE
(ex-N'castle, now Villa)

PETER WARD
(Brighton)

STRIKE
GOAL-GRABBERS WHO'RE A

GARRY BIRTLES
(Nottingham Forest)

MIKE FLANAGAN
(Crystal Palace)

KENNY DALGLISH
(Liverpool)

BRIAN KIDD
(Ex-Everton, now Bolton)

FORCE
MENACE TO EVERY DEFENCE

ALAN SUNDERLAND
(Arsenal)

STAN CUMMINS
(Sunderland)

ANDY GRAY
(Wolves)

'I'M NOT WORTH

KEVIN HIRD — ace defender

WHEN I put pen to paper to complete my £350,000 transfer from Blackburn Rovers to Leeds United in March, 1979, it ended a two month chase that had me linked with several First Division sides, Leeds, Everton and Manchester City among them.

I found it hard to believe so many Division One teams were showing interest. I couldn't help but think how different a story it was when I was 15.

At that age schoolboys are often invited for trials by senior clubs. But nobody ever contacted me.

It was my elder brother Kenneth who persuaded me to do it all off my own bat. I wrote for trials to all the local sides like Blackburn, Burnley, Blackpool and Bury.

The first reply came from Ewood Park. I went for a trial and three days later I signed schoolboy forms for Blackburn.

Kenneth has been the biggest influence on my career. I think that's because he can see in me what he wanted to do.

IN THE SPOTLIGHT

His ambition was to be a professional footballer. But he broke a leg in a motor-bike accident and his career never took off after that. He tried to help me make the most of my ability, too. He didn't want me to miss out as he had done.

Things didn't happen very quickly. I was a winger at the time and made reasonable progress through Blackburn's Lancashire League side, then into the reserves.

I have never been the most confident of blokes and it was holding me back.

Everything changed when the then Rovers' manager Jim Smith asked me to fill in at right-back against Burnley in December 1976.

I'd never thought of playing as a full-back, but everything just seemed to go right when I swopped positions.

The following season Blackburn did really well in the Second Division. We were chasing promotion most of the time and eventually ended up in fifth place.

It put the club in the spotlight and people started talking about Rovers' two attacking full-backs, myself and John Bailey (now with Everton).

All this made me a bit unsettled. It was something I had never thought about. I'd never con-

THAT!'

—Leeds' KEVIN HIRD talks about his big-money move

sidered being good enough to join a First Division team.

However, when you begin to read your name linked with top clubs you realise the chance is there. I heard that a big outfit had finally agreed a fee for me.

It seemed an eternity before I was told it was Leeds United who had made the offer.

Only weeks earlier my brother, Kenneth, had asked me if I fancied joining Manchester City, who at that particular time were showing most interest.

I told him if I had a choice it would be Elland Road! I was flabbergasted when I realised I had got that chance.

When I was told the fee Jimmy Adamson was going to pay for me, my first thought was—they must be mad!

I could not take it in that someone was prepared to pay £350,000 for me.

I couldn't believe I was worth that!

PRESSURE!

I immediately put pressure on myself. I kept saying "I'm going to have to give them something to prove I'm worth it."

However, after I'd signed, Leeds boss Jimmy Adamson took a certain amount of the pressure off me. He said that I had nothing at all to prove to him. I was to go out and play as normal. I did well in the remaining games of that season.

But at the start of last season I couldn't get into my game, I don't know whether it was a little bit of reaction setting in. Anyhow, I was dropped.

I pride myself these days that being dropped doesn't make me unsettled or perturbed. Instead it gives me an " I'll show 'em " attitude.

When I came back into the first-team I was moved into the midfield. I had played in the midfield for Blackburn before being converted to a full-back.

I felt after playing regularly for two years in the No. 2 shirt and Leeds paying all that money for me as a right-back, I could call myself a full-back. But now I'm not so sure what to call myself.

Signing for Leeds gave me my first real taste of European football. At Blackburn the only soccer I had played on the Continent was on a club holiday to Majorca.

We played a team of Spanish waiters. Our manager at the time, Gordon Lee, was in goal and we won 20-0!

Playing for a big club like Leeds United you might think I had great ambitions about getting to Wembley, lifting every trophy possible.

Yes, it would be nice, but I have never been a person to hold great ambitions.

I have in fact been to Wembley. But not as a fan or to play there.

Before the Centenary FA Cup final in 1972 there was a parade around the pitch to mark the occasion. Every side that had won the FA Cup was represented by apprentices.

As Blackburn Rovers had won the trophy on six occasions they had six apprentices in the parade. I was one of them. Paul Bradshaw (now with Wolves) carried the Rovers flag.

It was a fantastic day out. Something I will never forget. The atmosphere and noise when we walked down the tunnel was unbelievable.

I thought at the time what an even bigger thrill it must be emerging on to the pitch as one of the players of the participating sides . . . maybe one day.

JOHN BAILEY — attacking full-back

PETAR BOROTA
Chelsea

PETER EASTOE
Everton

DAVE WATSON hooks the ball clear from Bulgaria's ZHELYUKOV

DAVE WATSON as a goalscorer as he scores against Bulgaria.

TREVOR FRANCIS (left) and KEVIN REEVES on the alert in the goalmouth.

TONY WOODCOCK (right) scores against N. Ireland.

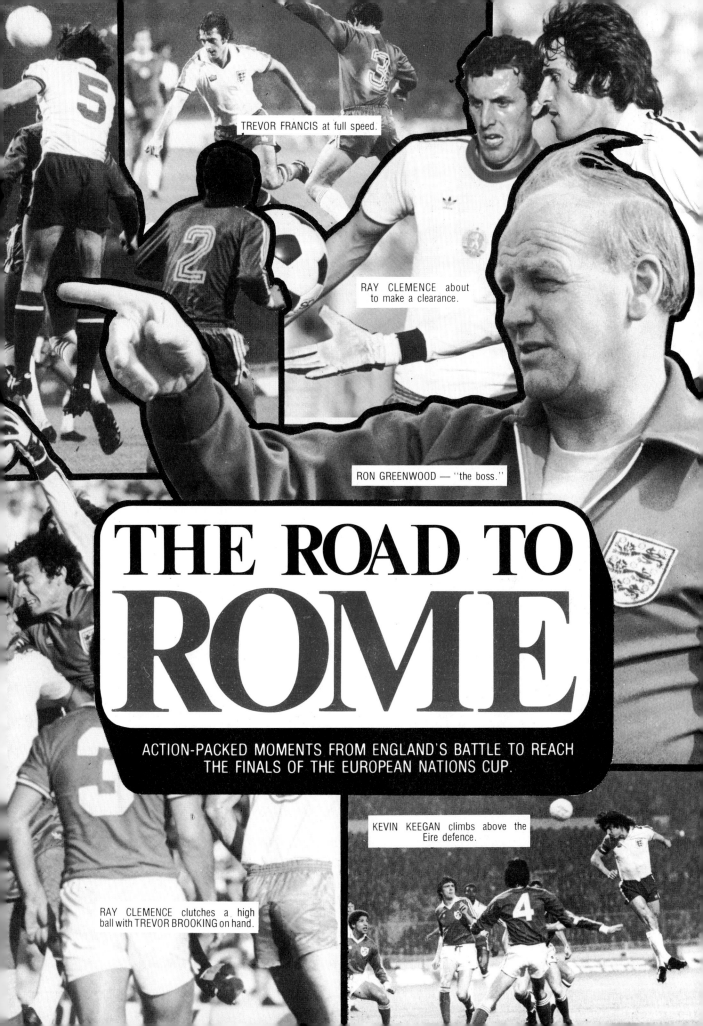

TREVOR FRANCIS at full speed.

RAY CLEMENCE about to make a clearance.

RON GREENWOOD — "the boss."

THE ROAD TO ROME

ACTION-PACKED MOMENTS FROM ENGLAND'S BATTLE TO REACH THE FINALS OF THE EUROPEAN NATIONS CUP.

KEVIN KEEGAN climbs above the Eire defence.

RAY CLEMENCE clutches a high ball with TREVOR BROOKING on hand.

TREVOR CHERRY
Leeds United

108

STEVE HARDWICK
Newcastle United

109

I'LL STAYA STOPPER

...Vows
Middlesbrough's
Defensive Strong Man—
BILLY ASHCROFT

STUART BOAM—
Wearing the Middlesbrough jersey that
Billy Ashcroft took over.

MOST players can put their finger on one incident and say . . . "That was the turning point of my career." I'm no exception.

It happened at the beginning of last season following two miserable and forgettable years with Middlesbrough.

I'd been bought from Wrexham for £130,000, then a record fee for 'Boro, to score goals. But the 14 I'd amassed in those 24 months said it all.

As a striker in the First Division Billy Ashcroft was something less than mediocre. To be honest, I was a bit of a flop.

In fact, I'd reached the stage where I simply couldn't afford another disastrous season at Ayresome Park.

I knew as the campaign approached that in the coming nine months I'd be playing not only for my future as a Middlesbrough player, but for my career as a player in top flight football.

What I didn't know was that just round the corner was a 'move' that was to turn my fortunes upside down.

Anyway, come the opening day of the season, the boss, John Neal, told me I was playing centre-half against 'Spurs in place of injured team skipper Stuart Boam.

I'd played at the back a few times during my Wrexham days when John Neal was boss at the Racecourse Ground. But, as then, I thought it was only an emergency matter.

There was no way I was honestly prepared for what did happen.

Within a matter of weeks what I could only consider a stop-gap role had opened up a whole new career.

The boss told me that my future now lay as a centre-half. And, as if to prove it, he duly sold Stuart Boam to Newcastle United.

It was a 'transfer' that caused a few raised eyebrows in the North East, I can tell you. But, personally, I could only regard it as the biggest compliment ever paid to me.

For a start 'Boamie' had become something of an institution at Ayresome. He was also reckoned to be among the best uncapped defenders in the country.

To be considered good enough to take over from him after barely a handful of games in the position was a bit of a dream.

But it was no dream. The weekly team sheet cried out that Billy Ashcroft was a First Division centre-half. And I was the last bloke complaining.

It would be wrong to say I took to the 'job' like a duck to water. At first it was a bit strange. There were bound to be one or two teething problems adapting to such a change in 'duties'.

You see, for quite some time I'd thought that

maybe one day I would become a goal-stopper as opposed to a goalscorer.

A striker's career normally doesn't stretch much beyond the age of 30. There aren't many who stay at the top long after that.

Defenders, however, seem to go on that bit longer. And I'd always thought that around the 30 mark I might be able to prolong my career a few years by moving back to defence.

As it's worked out I've made the 'move' quite a bit ahead of time. I'm still only 27. Now I reckon I can look forward to at least another five years in the top-flight . . . given the right breaks.

But, really, whatever success I get out of soccer I'll always be very grateful to manager John Neal. He has been the biggest single influence on my career.

It was John Neal who signed me for Wrexham, and who stuck by me when I went through a bad time at the Racecourse Ground. And it was he who gave me my First Division chance with Middlesbrough.

That's why I felt as if I'd really let him down in those dark early days.

He gambled a lot of money on me for long enough it must have appeared that he'd backed a loser. I was nobody's hero at Ayresome Park.

But, though he must obviously have been bitterly disappointed, he stuck by me again through all the lean times. Gave me the confidence to keep plugging away.

Now I believe I'm beginning to repay him and I intend to keep on doing so for a few years yet— as centre-half.

BRYAN ROBSON
West Bromwich Albion

112

FIESTA FOR FOOTBALL
—THAT'S ESPANA '82

THE European Championship is ended. Now International football is all about qualifying for Spain, 1982.

There will be twenty-four teams in Spain, compared with the sixteen that have competed in the final stages since the 1950 World Cup in Brazil.

By the time the qualifying matches are completed a Spanish orange will be set to become the most famous fruit in the world. In red shirt, blue shorts, black and green boots and holding a black and white ball. The mascot for 1982—Naranjito.

Any British team that reaches the Finals will be assured support. Already travel companies are beginning to work out trips that will combine a holiday in the sun with the finals of football's top competition.

Spain, who sent a team of experts to the Argentine to study the 1978 World Cup, are expected to spend between £40 and £60 million on improvements at the grounds which are to house the matches.

The aim is to spread the twenty four qualifying teams over a bigger area than any previous World Cup, covering fourteen separate centres.

The main grounds will be the Bernabeu Stadium in Madrid and the Nou Camp Stadium in Barcelona. Then add names like Valencia, Elche, Alicante, Zaragoza, Bilbao, Valladolid, Coruna, Vigo, Gijon, Malaga, Seville and Oviedo.

ESPANA **82**

Already the traditional rivalry between Madrid and Barcelona is starting. Barcelona have the opening match, but Madrid will have the Final.

In Madrid the capacity is expected to be only 90,000—all seated. Real Madrid believe that the future of football lies in all seated stadia.

They make the point that no stadium in the world constructed in the last ten years has approached a capacity of 100,000. The top capacity in the Argentine was 77,000. In West Germany, 84,000

Real's plans are to convert the 70,000 standing places on the terraces into around 45,000 seats. Added to the 45,649 seats already available this would give seating for over 90,000 under cover.

Barcelona go the other way. They are planning to spend £7 million to increase the capacity of the Nou Camp Stadium from 100,000 to 120,000.

They intend to add a third 'tier' to the stadium. That would give more standing room —as against the real Madrid all-seating plan.

Spain, 1982, is expected to be the best organised World Cup. A country already geared for tourists, they expect no problems about hotel accommodation. They are certain they can offer football fans the best of all worlds.

A holiday atmosphere, combined with the No. 1 football occasion—a real football fiesta.

K

FOOTBALL -IT'S A GREAT LIFE!

Says Celtic's ROY AITKEN

I CAN still see the look on the head-master's face.

"You want time off school to do what?" he slowly repeated, obviously hoping he hadn't heard me properly the first time.

To play in the European Cup-Winners' Cup with Celtic in East Germany, I told him.

In the year since I had joined up at Parkhead, the head had been used to some strange requests from me, but even he was shaken by that one.

Things were sorted out to everyone's satisfaction and so I, a seventeen-year-old school-boy, flew out with men like Kenny Dalglish, Bobby Lennox, and Danny McGrain to do battle in Europe.

So much has happened to me since then, it's hard to imagine that was only four years ago. I suppose that's one reason why I'm known as the youngest veteran in Scotland.

But I can tell you no matter what happens in my footballing career from now on, it's unlikely to be as eventful or unbelievable as those first few years.

For instance, I didn't play my first game of football until I was THIRTEEN, yet three years later I had made my debut in the Celtic first team, after asking the headmaster for the day off school, of course.

In between, I had played for Scotland Under-15 schoolboys as a left-back, and turned down the chance of another cap. Though this time at basketball which for a time was my number one sport.

I was chosen to play against Greece in Athens, but the game clashed with my first stint of pre-season training at Parkhead.

Well, by this time I had definitely decided that football was going to be my career, so I had to turn down the basketball invitation.

With that training under my belt, my career at Parkhead really began to take off. Though I was offered the chance to go full-time, I decided that it would be better to get some qualifications behind me—which led to problems, like that trip to East Germany. And getting time off school was the EASY part.

The Celtic boss at the time, Jock Stein, had actually to write to the authorities in Germany and tell them he was bringing a minor into the country.

WHEN FOOTBALL TOOK A BACK SEAT

Though they accepted that, they insisted that I have a personal bodyguard throughout my stay.

In actual fact, I don't know if I was shadowed, but I certainly didn't see anyone. Perhaps they used 007 himself.

Thankfully, not all of the highlights of my career so far have been off the field, and I've managed to win a few medals as well. More in fact than many players probably win in their whole life.

And no-one need remind me of just how lucky I've been in that respect. I know players who've been in the game longer than me, yet have nothing to show for their efforts. Yet here I am, just turned 22 with a handful of medals.

If I'm ever tempted to get a bit too big for my boots, that fact alone will bring me back down to earth with a bump.

And though it's been said many times before, there's no chance I'll ever think I've done it all and have nothing more to learn. And for that I can thank my travelling companion — a youngster called Bobby Lennox.

Ever since I joined Celtic, Bobby, who's a near neighbour of mine in Saltcoats, in Ayrshire, has travelled to and from Parkhead with me every day.

He's helped my career a lot, and one thing I've noticed is he's never afraid to listen to advice from others . . . and take note of it.

If that kind of attitude is good enough for a man like Bobby, who has been playing top class football for years, then it's certainly good enough for a beginner like me.

Not that Billy McNeill or anyone else at Parkhead is likely to let me think any other way, of course.

Mention of the boss brings me nicely to a question I'm often asked by fans. What position do you like playing best?

Billy, of course, has never hidden the fact that he sees my future in the team as a sweeper, but so far injuries and such like have meant I've had little chance to get used to the position.

I actually made my debut as a right-back, but I've played at centre-half, was capped as a left-back, and more recently I've been in midfield. Believe me, I don't care where I play.

I want to be involved with Celtic for years to come, and no matter what position I'm asked to play, I'll be quite happy.

Though I've had a fair deal of success so far, there are still a lot of things I'd like to do in football. Most of them not unnaturally connected with winning things.

I was absolutely thrilled when I won my first cap against Portugal in last season's European Championship, and I'd like to add to that for starters. Particularly after my experience when I had to pass up an international appearance I mentioned earlier.

To cut a long story short, combining football and study didn't work out as well as I had hoped, with the result I didn't do as well in my exams as I should have.

But one pass I was determined to get was in English, so after I signed full time, I kept up my studies at night school.

Fine so far. That is until the date of the exam reached me. When I checked my diary, I found that the date clashed with what would have been my fourth cap at Under-21 level. And it was against England at that.

Obviously I couldn't be in two places at one time, so I had to decide on exam or football. And for once, the latter took a back seat.

BOBBY LENNOX —

*with ten
of his eleven
championship
medals*

I would also like to win a European competition with Celtic. I'm not old enough to have seen most of the great side which won the European Cup in 1967 actually play, but I've heard thousands of stories about them, and they've made me determined to try to emulate them if possible.

By beating the mighty Real Madrid 2-0 at Parkhead last season, the present side showed just what they are capable of, and though we eventually lost that tie by the odd goal on aggregate, the experience has done most of the players the world of good and will help enormously this year.

A year, incidentally, in which I'll be trying to improve a bit on my field record.

I'm known as a hard man in many circles, and though I resent that title, I'm the first to admit that I don't hold back when I tackle.

At this point I'll let you into a little secret about a side of Roy Aitken which few people know about.

Opposition fans have called me a choice of names over the past few years, so I'll surprise them by telling them that the same Roy Aitken has a certificate from the London College of Music—in, whisper it, classical piano!

As I say, I realise I've been luckier than most people of my age, and football has given me a life style which many would envy. Football has certainly been good to me!

Liverpool's trophy display, telling the story of success and still more success. Cups, shields, pennants and all kinds of silverware, sure signs of a great team on the winning way.

ANFIELD'S

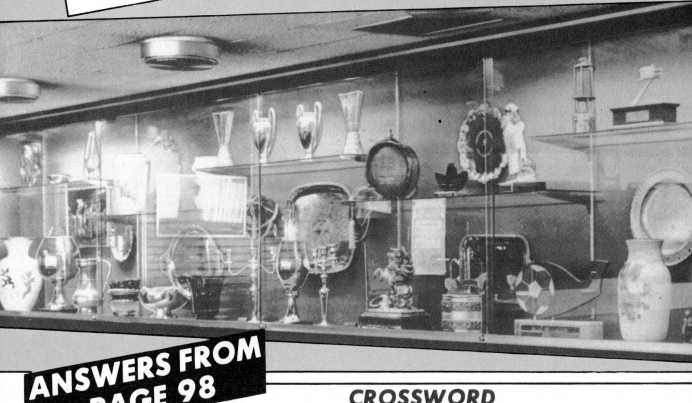

ANSWERS FROM PAGE 98

HOW DID YOU SCORE?

PICK A TEAM—

1 Peyton, 2 Rice, 3 Cannon, 4 Hansen,
5 Paddon, 6 Bowles, 7 Shoulder,
8 Brazil, 9 Jordan, 10 Carr, 11 Villa.

PICK A LETTER—

1 TurF, 2 HotspuR, 3 DenyA,
4 McGraiN, 5 CeltiC, 6 Macarl,
7 BirtleS. Missing player —FRANCIS.

TEAM TWISTERS—

1 Wigan Athletic, 2 Preston North End,
3 Bristol Rovers, 4 Hartlepool United, 5 Middlesbrough.

CROSSWORD

¹S		²M		³S		⁴C		⁵S		⁶W
⁷C	R	E	W	E		⁸R	A	N	G	E	R	S
O		D		M		A		A		S
⁹R	E	A	D	I	N	G		¹⁰G	A	T	E	¹¹S
E		L		G		H				H		E
			¹²D	O	N	S		¹⁴O	H	A	R	E
¹⁵D		¹⁶S		L		O		W		M		D
¹⁷E	W	O	O	D		¹⁸H	I	L	L
L		U				O			¹⁹S		²⁰L
²¹L	Y	N	C	²²H		²³D	E	B	A	²⁴C	L	E
		T		E		U		D		U		O		E
²⁵A	R	S	E	N	A	L		²⁶R	A	T	E	D	S
		S		T		E		Y		S		S		S

ALADDIN'S CAVE...

LETTER LINKS—

Hartford, Coppell, Jennings, Thomas, Kennedy, Wilkins, Brooking, Latchford, Cherry, Provan.

H	A	V	O	R	P	E	H	D	G	N	I
O	T	R	A	N	Y	R	C	R	L	K	O
R	F	N	I	N	R	E	O	A	T	O	B
C	D	N	E	G	K	N	F	H	C	R	S
P	O	J	L	S	O	S	N	Y	L	K	N
P	E	L	T	H	M	A	E	D	W	I	Y

PYRAMID CUBES.

```
                    R
              ¹R    A    Y
          ²B   O    N    D   S
      ³H   U   N    G    A   R   Y
  ⁴H   E   N   D    E    R   S   O   N
⁵D   U   N   F   E    R    M   L   I   N   E
⁶L  E   Y   T   O   N    S    T   A   D   I   U   M
```

STEVE HUNT
Coventry City

BYRON'S ON THE BALL!

BALL balancing skill that any seal would envy — that's one of the talents of Byron Stevenson of Leeds and Wales.

On nose or fingertips Byron can spin a full-sized football in an amazing display of ball-juggling.

And he's proved for club and country that he's pretty nifty with his feet, too.

GET UP – AND GRIT YOUR TEETH!

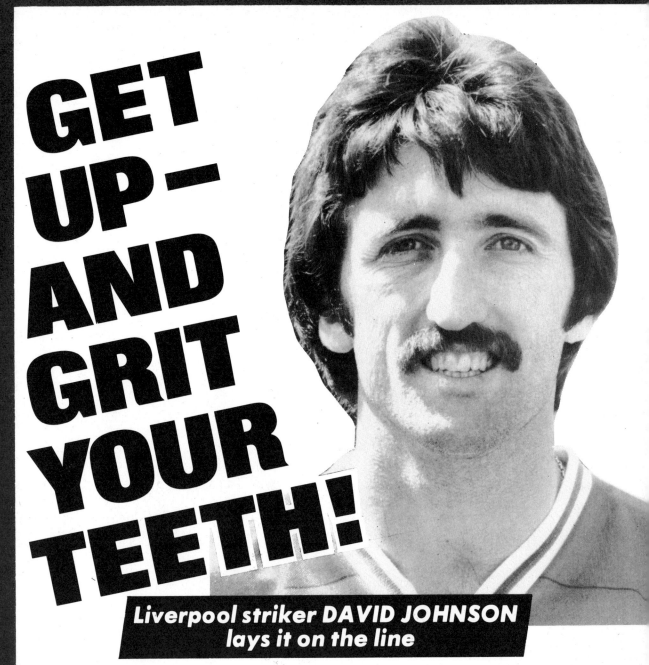

Liverpool striker DAVID JOHNSON lays it on the line

I HAVE always wanted to wear the white shirt of England. I never gave up the chase even when I was kicking my heels in reserve team football.

That is why last season was the greatest experience of my life.

I won a First Division Championship medal with my home town club Liverpool—and I got a recall to the England squad.

I travelled a few miles to get there. I left the other great Merseyside club Everton to sign for Ipswich across country in East Anglia.

I made that move because I felt Ipswich were a team that would win something big—and that would set me up for a chance with England. It worked, too.

I was picked for my country and I thought I had made the grade. But football will always come up with disappointments and I soon faded out of the picture.

It was then I heard that Liverpool wanted me. I could hardly believe my luck. The most successful team in the land and I was the man they wanted to join their attack!

I jumped at the chance even though I was told there would be no automatic first team place. Kevin Keegan and John Toshack were still going strong. But I felt that if I waited I would get into the side—and a Liverpool first team place is the best ticket you can get for international football.

I was so wrong. I picked up two very bad injuries and I couldn't break out of the reserve side. I was so miserable I even went to talk terms with Leicester City when they made an offer for me.

As it turned out I did the right thing by turning them down and setting my mind on one last effort to prove to Liverpool I could do the job.

I got my opportunity two seasons back—and to my delight the goals started to hit the back of the net.

For a Scouser like me there is no better feeling in the world than scoring a goal for Liverpool in front of my own folk.

My fitness came back and my speed built up. I felt so good some days I thought I could fly. Then England boss Ron Greenwood gave me a call—the message I had been longing to hear. I can't say it has all been joy. In my first game back I broke my cheekbone at Wembley and was carried off.

In Liverpool's F.A. Cup semi-final against Arsenal I took another whack on the head and had stitches over and below my right eye.

Both my injuries were close to the eye and I can tell you I was very frightened as I lay on the turf waiting for the trainer.

And the next game back you find yourself thinking twice before you put your head to a ball with a big centre-half.

That's the side they don't tell you about when you are told what a wonderful career you can have in football.

It's a battle all the time to keep your nerve and your determination to win the ball. You can't teach a young boy that nerve. He must have a steely desire to get into the thick of things—and

DAVID JOHNSON — on target for England

go back again even when he gets carted off with a bad injury.

That is part of the secret that keeps Liverpool on top. We very seldom lose players for many games.

At Anfield they pick themselves up and get on with the game. That same determination goes into the running. When your chest is heaving and your legs ache it is tempting to stand back and let someone else do the chasing. But he could be feeling as bad as you do. If you both stand back—nothing!

It kept us going last season when results began to go wrong at a vital stage in the season. We eventually lost to Arsenal in the semi-final after four games. We still had three points to collect in the league to win the title and we could have claimed tiredness and disappointment.

At Liverpool these words are looked upon as excuses. We rolled up our sleeves and grabbed the points that killed off the challenge from Manchester United.

Striker for England and the champions of the First Division. Sounds very glamorous, doesn't it? I won't deny I love all the excitement—but never forget that the real test comes when you are lying in pain feeling you can't run another step.

That is when you find out if you have got what it takes to stay at the top. If you get up and grit your teeth you have got a chance in football.

STEVE DALEY
Manchester City

122

IT HAPPENED LAST SEASON

1. Liverpool players came first, second and third in the PFA 'Player of the Year' awards. Who were they and in what order?

2. Who were the first and last clubs to know they had been promoted?

See question 5.

3. He became the most expensive teenager in football when he signed for a First Division side for over £1,000,000. His name and the clubs involved, please.

4. Who was Scotland's Sportswriters' Player of the Year?

5. Ipswich Town 'keeper Paul Cooper set up an amazing sequence of penalty saves. Only two kicks evaded him in ten attempts. Name the scorers of those two spot-kicks.

6. Which player scored a hat-trick on his England Under-21 debut?

7. Wales acquired a new team manager. Name him and the club former boss Mike Smith took over.

8. Which 'keeper saved three penalties in one match and still ended up losing 6-0?

9. Name Scotland's top goalscorer and his club.

10. Which non-League side went furthest in the FA Cup?

11. One side scored over a century of League goals. Name the side and their goal tally.

12. Name the only Scottish team to complete its League programme without a single away victory.

13. Who was the Football League's top scorer?

14. What record was set up when Sheffield Wednesday met Sheffield United at Hillsborough on Boxing Day?

15. Name the grounds used in the FA Cup semi-finals.

16. Which player made his League debut for two different clubs in the space of only two weeks?

17. Rangers and Dundee were the two clubs involved in the biggest ever transfer deal between two Scottish clubs. Who was the player?

18. Phil Boyer knocked home 26 goals in all competitions. But how many were scored away from home?

19. Which foreign player became the first import to be transferred between English clubs?

20. Name the player who became the youngest ever FA Cup finalist.

21. Which side ended Nottingham Forest's run of 51 unbeaten League games at the City Ground?

22. The highest win of the League season was an 8-0 scoreline achieved in the Third Division. Name the sides please.

Answers on page 125

JOHN HAWLEY
Sunderland

YOUR PICTURE GUIDE

Colour

Action

Pin-ups

Groups

Portraits

QUIZ ANSWERS
from page 123

1 — 1st, Terry McDermott; 2nd, David Johnson; 3rd, Kenny Dalglish.
2 — Walsall and Sunderland.
3 — Clive Allen (Q.P.R. to Arsenal).
4 — Gordon Strachan (Aberdeen).
5 — Gerry Francis (Crystal Palace) and Kevin Hird (Leeds Utd.)
6 — Garth Crooks (Stoke City).
7 — Mike England and Hull City.
8 — Gary Bailey (Manchester U.).
9 — Doug Somner (St Mirren).
10 — Harlow Town.
11 — Huddersfield T. (101 goals).
12 — Hibernian.
13 — Clive Allen (Q.P.R., now Arsenal) 28 goals.
14 — Highest-ever Third Division attendance (49,309).
15 — Hillsborough, Villa Park (three times), Elland Road and Highfield Road.
16 — Asa Hartford for Nottingham Forest and Everton.
17 — Ian Redford.
18 — Three goals.
19 — Alex Sabella (Sheffield United to Leeds United).
20 — Paul Allen (West Ham Utd.)
21 — Brighton.
22 — Swindon beat Bury.

Printed and published by D. C. Thomson & Co. Ltd., 185 Fleet Street, London EC4A 2HS.
© D. C. Thomson & Co. Ltd., 1980.
ISBN 0 85116 196 0